OLD TESTAMENT GUIDES

General Editor
R.N. Whybray

LEVITICUS

LEVITICUS

Lester L. Grabbe

Sheffield Academic Press

First Published by Sheffield Academic Press 1993
Reprinted 1997

Copyright © 1993, 1997 Sheffield Academic Press

Published by Sheffield Academic Press Ltd
Mansion House
19 Kingfield Road
Sheffield S11 9AS
England

Printed on acid-free paper in Great Britain
by The Cromwell Press
Melksham, Wiltshire

British Library Cataloguing in Publication Data

A catalogue record for this book is available
from the British Library

ISBN 1-85075-440-3

Contents

Abbreviations

AB	Anchor Bible
AnBib	Analecta biblica
BA	*Biblical Archaeologist*
BBB	Bonner biblische Beiträge
BJS	Braun Judaic Studies *Bib Biblica*
BKAT	Biblischer Kommentar: Altes Testament
CBQ	*Catholic Biblical Quarterly*
E-I	*Eretz Israel*
FRLANT	Forschungen zur Religion und Literatur des Alten und Neuen Testaments
HAT	Handbuch zum Alten Testament
HSM	Harvard Semitic Monographs
HUCA	*Hebrew Union College Annual*
IDBSup	*Interpreter's Dictionary of the Bible, Supplementary Volume*
JBL	*Journal of Biblical Literature*
JCS	*Journal of Cuneiform Studies*
JNES	*Journal of Near Eastern Studies*
JQR	*Jewish Quarterly Review*
JSJ	*Journal for the Study of Judaism*
JSOT	*Journal for the Study of the Old Testament*
LCL	Loeb Classical Library
NICOT	New International Commentary on the Old Testament
OTL	Old Testament Library
OTS	Oudtestamentische Studiën
RB	*Revue biblique*
SBL	Society of Biblical Literature
SC	Sources Chrétiennes
SJLA	Studies in Judaism in Late Antiquity
VT	*Vetus Testamentun*
VTSup	*Vetus Testamentum,* Supplements
WMANT	Wissenschaftliche Monographien zum Alten und Neuen Testament
ZAW	*Zeitschrift für die alttestamentliche Wissenschaft*

Select List of Commentaries

Major commentaries on Leviticus include the following:

K. Elliger, *Leviticus* (HAT 4; Tübingen: Mohr [P. Siebeck], 1966). Extensive literary criticism of the text.

J. Milgrom, *Leviticus 1–16* (AB 3; Garden City, NY: Doubleday, 1991). With over 1000 pages in volume I alone, this will no doubt become one of the major commentaries on the book.

M. Noth, *Leviticus: A Commentary* (OTL; London: SCM Press, 1977). A classic commentary, very readable for students, with emphasis on the traditio-historical approach.

J.R. Porter, *Leviticus* (Cambridge Bible Commentary on the New English Bible; Cambridge: Cambridge University Press, 1976). Aimed more at the non-specialist.

R. Rendtorff, *Leviticus* (BKAT III; Neukirchen–Vluyn: Neukirchener Verlag, 1985–). Only two fascicles are available, up to Leviticus 5.

G.J. Wenham, *The Book of Leviticus* (NICOT; Grand Rapids: Eerdmans, 1979). A conservative Christian perspective.

For the literary and form criticism of the book and general questions on the growth of the book, see the following, in addition to the major commentaries:

A. Cholewinski, *Heiligkeitsgesetz und Deuteronomium* (AnBib 66, Rome: Pontifical Biblical Institute, 1976).

R. Kilian, *Literarkritische und formgeschichtliche Untersuchung des Heiligkeitsgesetzes* (BBB 19; Bonn: Peter Hanstein, 1963).

K. Koch, *Die Priesterschrift von Exodus 25 bis Leviticus 16: Eine überlieferungsgeschichtliche und literarische Untersuchung* (FRLANT 71; Göttingen: Vandenhoeck & Ruprecht, 1959).

I. Knohl, 'The Priestly Torah Versus the Holiness School: Sabbath and the Festivals', *HUCA* 58 (1987), pp. 65-117.

M. Noth, *A History of Pentateuchal Traditions* (Englewood Cliffs, NJ: Prentice–Hall, 1972).

R. Rendtorff, *Die Gesetze in der Priesterschrift: Eine gattungsgeschichtliche Untersuchung* (Göttingen: Vandenhoeck & Ruprecht, 2nd edn, 1963).

H. Graf Reventlow, *Das Heiligkeitsgesetz formgeschichtlich untersucht* (WMANT; Neukirchen–Vluyn: Neukirchener Verlag, 1961).

1

INTRODUCTION

NO OTHER BOOK OF THE BIBLE is less appealing, at first sight, to the modern student of theology than Leviticus. With its detailed regulations about the sacrificial cult, it seems irrelevant to many. The traditional Christian polemic has tended to label such practices as 'meaningless ritual'. To vegetarians and those arguing for animal rights, the concept of blood sacrifice may seem downright barbaric. So why should this book be of interest to Christians and Jews today?

Yet Jesus' famous statement that one should love one's neighbour as oneself (Mk 12.31) is, actually, a quotation from Lev. 19.18. And Jewish and Christian commentators through the centuries have found Leviticus an important source of religious symbolism and theological reflection. Far from being devoted to 'empty ritual', Leviticus presupposes an ethical system in the sacrificial structure which it outlines. There is much more to the book than sacrifices, though the information in it is vital for the understanding of worship in ancient Israel and in the temple until its destruction in 70 CE.

When people discuss religion and its practice, there is often a tacit assumption that religion is subsumed under ethics; this is a mistake. Ethics is only one aspect of religion; and, on the other hand, there can be an ethical system without religion, as many atheists have pointed out. In the practice of Judaism and Christianity there is much which has no direct concern with ethics: the nature of the divine, prayer, proper worship, love and respect for God, removal of sin, the atonement; these are primarily theological questions, not ethical ones. The appropriate forms of worship are matters of concern to all religious people, however much they may dispense with formalized ritual. Leviticus is as seriously concerned with the right way of worshipping God as are the psalms and prophets.

So, there are a number of reasons why Leviticus remains important today: (1) it forms a part of the Bible of both Christians and Jews; (2) the sacrificial cult was at the centre of the worship of Yahweh in ancient Israel, and no proper comprehension of Israelite religion is possible without recognizing this fact; (3) recent anthropological study has found purity and pollution, community rituals, sacrifice and other cultic activities to be valuable in understanding the functioning of pre-industrial societies; (4) there is more to Leviticus than cultic ritual, including such topics as repentance, forgiveness of sin, relations between the sexes, and social justice. A closer look at the text reveals many fascinating points and insights into society, history, religion, and theology.

Leviticus and the 'Priestly Source'

The 'documentary hypothesis' or 'Graf–Wellhausen hypothesis' has dominated study of the Pentateuch for the past century. According to that theory, most of Leviticus belongs to the priestly source (P), though the P writers may have used a range of material in composing it. For example, many would see chs. 17–26 (usually referred to as H, for the holiness code) as a separate block of material originally, which was taken over by P. The traditional dating of P was the exilic period, in the middle of the sixth century BCE.

In recent years, however, there have been two challenges to this consensus: it has been questioned (1) whether P should not be dated to the pre-exilic period, and (2) whether the traditional sources exist at all. Although biblical fundamentalists have continually rejected the documentary hypothesis for dogmatic reasons, it should not be assumed that recent challenges fall into that same category. Even if some of the arguments have been voiced for a long time, many of those who now oppose the old consensus do so for critical reasons which have nothing to do with a desire to 'defend' the biblical text.

Dating of P
The traditional scholarly consensus began, primarily, with Wellhausen, who dated P partly on the basis of an assumed development of Israelite religion. He saw it as the formalization of an originally spontaneous form of worship, though he also recognized other criteria. Since Wellhausen's time, this dating to the sixth century—whether the exilic or the early post-exilic period—has remained fairly constant among critics. An exception was Vink who put it in the fourth century, but few have followed him. It is generally agreed that the sixth century is the date of the final form of the work, although the editor/author drew on various priestly traditions, some of them of substantial antiquity.

A major deviation from this consensus was proposed by Y. Kaufmann. He dated P well into the pre-exilic period, even earlier than the deuteronomic stratum (D). For some time his thesis stood alone, but a new scholarly trend has developed under his influence which questions the consensus from several angles. The challenge is based primarily on two grounds.

One of these is historical-literary and is represented by M. Haran, who argued for a situation similar to that postulated by Kaufmann. In his study, *Temples and Temple Service in Ancient Israel*, Haran examined the traditions about the wilderness tabernacle during Israel's supposed forty years wandering before entering the Promised Land. He attempted to show that many of these traditions actually relate to the period of the monarchy, sometimes to the early monarchy or even earlier. Thus, in his opinion, P is an ancient product of the priesthood; but because it was produced and preserved by the priests primarily for their own use, it is not clearly attested until after the reform of Josiah c. 620 BCE. (Josiah's reform is traditionally associated with Deuteronomy and the 'D' stratum of the Pentateuch.) However, it is much older and even formed the basis of the unsuccessful cultic reform of Hezekiah c. 700 BCE, almost a century before Josiah.

M. Weinfeld has approached the question from the point of view of Deuteronomy, first in his *Deuteronomy and the Deuteronomic School* and more recently in his commentary on Deuteronomy. He argued that P and D belong to two different circles or 'schools' with different social backgrounds and underlying ideologies. P arose in priestly circles and is theologically focused and sanctuary-centred. The regime of holiness, its sacred institutions, and its system of purity and pollution all belong to the time of the judges or the early monarchy and are attested in early Old Testament literature. D, on the other hand, arose in scribal circles and reflects more closely the realities of the secular court. While there are no direct links with P, it nevertheless depended, at some points, on priestly views and phraseology (for example, Deuteronomy 34 is reworked from priestly material).

Another argument used for dating P early is linguistic. This can be used in conjunction with the arguments of Kaufmann and Haran, but may be independent. In a series of articles and a monograph, A. Hurvitz concentrated on linguistic criteria. He argued that certain vocabulary used in P had become obsolete by the post-exilic period. Also, when the language of Ezekiel (traditionally dated to the exilic period) is compared with that of P, the language of the Priestly Source is clearly earlier. Ezekiel and other writings of the exile and post-exilic period show characteristics of the later stratum of the language known as Late Biblical Hebrew. More importantly, even though there are many ancient forms in P, in Hurvitz's opinion there are no exclusively late ones.

Not everyone has been convinced by Hurvitz's arguments. One contention (by Cross for example) is that the language of P is archaizing; in other words, the writer consciously attempted to imitate an older form of the language. In such cases, however, there are almost always some later forms reflecting the author's own time. Hurvitz attempted to deal with this question in a study comparing P and the language of Ezekiel. Another problem is whether P can be taken as a linguistic unity. For example, Rendtorff (who queries the existence of the P source on other grounds) thinks that the language of Leviticus is a special priestly jargon which cannot be dated to one specific period (one might compare the language of modern legal documents). Even Polzin, whose work is considered the main study on the subject, thinks that P has some of the linguistic characteristics of Late Biblical Hebrew. The linguistic debate will go on, and it is too soon to say what course it is likely to take. Interestingly, however, the old consensus that the language of P is late can no longer be maintained without significant argumentation.

Perhaps the most comprehensively argued thesis on the subject is that of Jacob Milgrom in his recent monumental commentary on Leviticus, in which he challenges a number of old ideas. On P specifically, he accepts the idea of the P source but argues that the core of it arose at an early time in Israel's history, shortly before the founding of the monarchy. It grew up primarily in association with the temple cult at Shiloh which preceded the kingship of David and the founding of the temple at Jerusalem. In this he is developing a thesis already advanced by Haran, but the detail with which he argues it is his own contribution. He thinks that certain portions of Leviticus are later editings, reflecting developments in the history of the cult. Nevertheless, the cult described in Leviticus is in the main that which was carried on at Shiloh before the temple in Jerusalem was founded.

In Milgrom's opinion, evidence for this comes from several considerations. The first is linguistic. Milgrom quotes from Hurvitz but adds further examples to show that the vocabulary of P is early; these include terms which dropped out of use long before the exile. On the other hand, he maintains that none of the key terms is demonstrably post-exilic. Therefore, P has not been archaized but is genuinely old (with the exception of some few post-exilic additions). Milgrom also argues that D is dependent on P and H rather than the other way round, though admittedly this is demonstrated only for the content and not the language of P. The dietary laws in particular, Milgrom maintains, provide evidence for D's dependence on P. One of the most striking examples among the many given is that Deut. 12.15, 21 permits non-sacrificial slaughter, whereas Leviticus 17.3-7 (H) limits the slaughter of domestic animals to the cult. It seems unlikely that D would have preceded P in this case.

Milgrom's *magnum opus* stands much scholarship on its head. Instead of being late, P was early; instead of relating to the Second Temple, it preceded even the First Temple; instead of being built on Deuteronomy, the Deuteronomists borrowed heavily from it. Finally the small temple 'state' presupposed by P is not the Persian province of Yehud but the tribal entity associated with Shiloh before Israel became a monarchy. The debate is set to run for many years, and we can do no more than introduce it here. Milgrom backs up his thesis with detailed textual arguments which cannot be dismissed in a few statements. If his thesis is refuted, it will be by careful attention to detail and lengthy argument; but he may change the shape of scholarship on P in general and on Leviticus in particular.

Was There a P Document?

As radical as a redating of P is the doubt over whether it ever existed as a documentary source of the Pentateuch. According to the Graf–Wellhausen thesis, P was an independent narrative document parallel to the Yahwistic and Elohistic (JE) strand(s). Wellhausen himself emphasized the narrative character of the document and thought that much of the cultic material of Leviticus was not a part of the original P source. Noth's view was similar, but he modified this by arguing that P came to an end before the end of Numbers and thus did not have a version of the settlement in the land. Elliger also thought that much of the cultic material in Leviticus was composed of later additions. Noth argued that P was the matrix of the Pentateuch into which the JE strands were edited, resulting in a definite P character and perspective for the final form of the Pentateuch. Another view is expressed by Koch, who considered the cultic material a part of the original P narrative, and others have made no distinction between the legal and the narrative sections (Hurvitz and Milgrom for example).

Recent challenges to the concept of an independent P document come in two forms. One questions the entire basis of the documentary hypothesis. These criticisms have nothing in common with those who have stubbornly maintained the Mosaic authorship of the Pentateuch because of their theological presuppositions. Indeed, some of the recent challengers would actually date much of the material of the Pentateuch later than does Wellhausen. An important criticism of the documentary hypothesis came from U. Cassuto but received little support. As a leading traditio-historical critic, Rendtorff was one of the originators of the current debate. He drew attention to the fact that certain blocks of material which were originally thought to be split between the sources JEP each have their own tradition history and unity.

R.N. Whybray in *The Making of the Pentateuch* examines the literary and traditio-historical proposals with regard to the Pentateuch, before concluding that they are all inadequate. Drawing on the insights of a number of recent studies, especially that of J. Van Seters, Whybray argues that a good analogy for the Pentateuch would be the roughly contemporary *Histories* of Herodotus. The Greek historian used many sources, some written and some oral, but he did not simply join them together like a patchwork quilt. Rather, he digested them and then made them a part of his own composition, with his own particular style. It would be difficult, if not impossible, to sort out Herodotus's sources, certainly not in the way proposed by the documentary hypothesis. The argument of Whybray and others is that sources have been too reworked and changed to be separated out again in the neat fashion hypothesised by the Graf–Wellhausen thesis. Thus, Whybray argues that, while there may have been a number of different sources, the idea of long narratives of J and E which can be reconstructed must now be abandoned.

The second challenge to the old consensus on P is to see it not as one of the documentary sources but as an editorial layer with particular characteristics. Calling into question the whole documentary hypothesis, Rendtorff argued that P was not a separate document but only an editorial layer in the tradition. Not all those who take a different view of P have questioned the entire documentary hypothesis, however. For example, Cross had already argued that P was a series of editings and supplements to JE rather than a separate document. This does not mean that it contains little new material: Rendtorff believes that a good deal of new material was added at this stage of redaction to create a new context and unity.

Throughout this book I shall refer to P when citing the material normally identified as part of the P document. However, in each case the reader should understand the qualifying phrase, 'if it exists' or 'as normally identified'. I have no intention of begging the question of whether P exists or, if it does, what it comprises.

Growth of Leviticus

The previous section may seem confusing to readers who come to Leviticus for the first time, but this is all to the good. It is important that students and non-specialists are aware that scholarship is rarely cut and dried. Even the existence of a consensus at one particular time does not settle the matter; further study may cause the old consensus to be rejected. It is not my intention to say who is right and wrong but rather to introduce arguments, to provide some guidance to the present state of scholarship and, above all, to challenge readers to dig into the text for themselves.

What can be said with confidence, however, is that the book of Leviticus has undergone a long period of growth, with many additions and editings; scholars are agreed on this point. It is also clear that much of the material within it derives from priestly circles: Leviticus is a 'priestly' document as it now stands, whether or not there was a P source as envisaged by the documentary hypothesis. There is agreement that Leviticus has a complicated tradition history.

More controversial are the precise stages of this growth. In recent years many different monographs and commentaries have attempted to tease out the different layers (see Rendtorff, Kilian, Koch, Milgrom). It is beyond my purpose to look at the different suggestions in detail, but some of the larger issues should be mentioned. Leviticus 17–26 is usually divided from the rest as the so-called holiness code (H). Not all agree with this delineation, but most would agree that within 17–26 is another document which has been incorporated but is not necessarily fully integrated with 1–16. That is to say, both 1–16 and 17–26 are collections with their own stages of growth, each with a relative unity in itself which marks it off from the other. There are tensions between the two parts, with some major differences of outlook on certain issues.

It is difficult to determine the relative dates of the two collections. In the past H was thought to be earlier than most of the material in 1–16. Breaking with the consensus, A. Cholewski concluded that H was actually later than 1–16. I. Knohl came to a similar conclusion, arguing on the basis of Leviticus 23 which, he maintained, was constructed on Numbers 28–29. Milgrom argues that most of H is later than most of 1–16, though in his opinion H was one of the editors of Leviticus itself (other additions were made by his editors P[2], P[3], P[4]). Apart from an extended discussion of Knohl's thesis, almost the only example Milgrom gives is 19.7-8 (H) which he thinks is dependent on 7.18 (P). This may be expanded on in future publications by Milgrom.

New Approaches and Methods

Noting the general consensus that the book grew over a long period of time, one might ask, 'What level of the book should be interpreted'? In recent years, many interpreters have argued for the final form of the biblical text as the primary object of study, whatever the stages of growth of the book or its dating may have been. This has led to the use of a number of new disciplines under the general rubric of the 'literary approach', including 'close reading', structuralism, deconstruction, and rhetorical criticism. So far, few have been applied to Leviticus specifically (but see Damrosch and Schwartz for examples). From a different perspective, those interested in the 'canonical' form for theological purposes are also concerned mainly with the final form of the text (see especially Childs).

This does not mean that the final form of the text has been ignored even by some of the traditional disciplines. For decades, many form critics have practised a structural analysis of the text as it reads now, before asking questions about growth or genre and the like. The results of this approach may be seen in the series *Forms of Old Testament Literature* edited by R.P. Knierim and G. Tucker. Knierim's recent book on exegesis combines traditional form criticism with broader concerns, including theological and sociological ones. Some exegetes, while not abandoning traditional source criticism, have demoted it in their concerns. For example, while Rendtorff does not reject 'reconstruction' of earlier phases of the tradition, he thinks that this should be used primarily as an aid to understanding the present text.

This does not suggest that older methods of source criticism and the like can be forgotten. On the contrary, they often lie beneath the new methods. Traditio-historical analysis is very important for two further legitimate stages of interpretation. A second level of interpretation is that of Leviticus as a part of the P document (see below); and yet a third object of interpretation would be the various levels in the growth of the book as determined by form and redaction criticism. This is the most hypothetical method and is less favoured today for that reason (cf. Rendtorff). However, most commentators give some attention to the internal growth of the book, and many see it as a primary concern.

Structure and Contents

The structure and contents of Leviticus will be dealt with by R.P. Knierim in his contribution to the *Forms of Old Testament Literature* series (Grand Rapids, MI: Eerdmans). For present purposes, they may be outlined as follows:

Sacrificial system	1–7
Introduction	1.1-2
Whole burnt offering	1.3-17
Cereal offering	2
Well-being offering	3
Sin offering	4–5
Normal sin offering	4
Scaled sin offering	5.1-13
Guilt offering	5.14-26 (Eng. 5.14–6.7)
Laws (*tôrôt*) of the offerings	6–7
Law of burnt offering	6.1-6 (6.8-13)
Law of cereal offering	6.7-11 (6.14-18)
Offering at Aaron's anointment	6.12-16 (6.19-23)

Relationship of Leviticus to the Actual Temple Cult

Does Leviticus (perhaps together with the rest of P) describe the rites in the temple, or is it merely a theoretical document, a programme, or even a fantasy? It may be said with some confidence that Leviticus does not describe the cult in a tabernacle built by the Israelites under Moses during the forty years in the wilderness. The whole story, as described in the biblical text (from Exodus to the end of Deuteronomy), is now generally rejected as unhistorical by biblical scholars. A generation ago, many would have given greater credence to the story, or at least to certain parts of it. New archaeological information and further study have convinced most scholars that Israel was not entered by a unified group out of the wilderness after escaping from Egypt. Rather, even if some people had been in Egypt, they would have been few in number. The bulk of those who came to make up Israel were probably indigenous people, though there may have been immigrants from outside the area. Those who coalesced to produce Israel no doubt had their shrines, permanent or portable, but the description of building the tabernacle in Exodus is fiction as it stands. Nevertheless, one may seek some reality that may have lain behind it.

The description in P may be purely hypothetical or utopian. Priests who had a vision of an idealized cult could write and present it as if that was what actually happened under Moses. There is no doubt that there is a certain amount of idealization in the description of the tabernacle and the setting up of its cult. However, most scholars would see some relationship between the text and the activities in an actual temple or shrine. Those who date P to the post-exilic period consider the priestly material to reflect, broadly, the situation in the Second Temple which was built in the early Persian period. If P is dated to the exilic period, one would expect it to present a programme for a renewed cult in Jerusalem (which was expected imminently), with the hope of influencing the structure of the new cult. On the other hand, Cross advanced the thesis that the tent of David, which housed the ark before and after its removal to Jerusalem before the temple was built, was the basis of the tabernacle tradition.

The revolutionary proposal of Haran and Milgrom relates the core of Leviticus to the temple at Shiloh in the early period of the monarchy. Milgrom points to three arguments which indicate a shrine with only a small territory and governed by a single priestly family: (1) the purification rite for the person with a discharge (*zav*) required a journey which could be completed in one day; (2) the thanksgiving offering was originally eaten by the offerer in the sanctuary grounds; (3) the priestly portions originally went to the presiding priest, whereas certain supplementary statements change that to the priests as a whole. Milgrom's argument concerns later editings which attempted to up-date the material, some of these being as late as the post-exilic period. Therefore, despite possible earlier origins, the cult and regulations in the present text of Leviticus can, in most cases, be related to the practice in the First Temple ascribed to Solomon: this argument also supports those who see the final form of P as dating from the post-exilic period.

Most accept that Leviticus, to a large extent, represents actual cultic practice, despite some tensions and contradictions. Editings there have been, perhaps because of changes and developments in actual practice. But it is also likely that many cultic procedures remained essentially unchanged over long periods. The many differences in detail between Leviticus and other passages in the Old Testament do not suggest major differences in the overall shape of the cult. Those who see Leviticus as largely a description of cultic observance in the Second Temple period are probably correct since, even if much of it goes back to the First Temple, the same practices were continued when the temple was rebuilt.

Law in Israel and the Ancient Near East

For a proper understanding of certain sections of Leviticus, it is important to have some introduction to the subject of law in the ancient Near East. A number of law codes from Mesopotamia have been discovered during the past century, in addition to many legal documents which describe judicial decisions made in regard to actual cases. The earliest law code so far known, and then only in fragments, is the Sumerian Ur-Nammu from about 2100 BCE. Others include Lipit-Ishtar (c. 1875 BCE), Eshnunna (c. 1750 BCE), Hammurabi (c. 1700 BCE), the Middle Assyrian Laws (twelfth century), and Hittite laws (c. thirteenth century). Little has come from Egypt, probably because of the different administrative structure. (The pharaoh was regarded as the author of law and order and this did not encourage the development of formal law codes.) The most famous, as well as the most extensive and developed of these law codes, is the Codex Hammurabi.

The relationship between the law codes and the actual legal documents is an interesting one which may throw light on the relationship of Old Testament law to its practice in Israel. It is by no means straightforward because the law codes were not, as one might expect, analogous to a statute book which judges would consult for information and guidance. On the contrary, actual legal decisions never refer to the law codes as precedent or as authoritative legislation (for a different opinion see Westbrook). The judges may have relied on a common law tradition, some other guide or even their own common sense, but their decisions show no explicit knowledge of the law codes, although in some cases these were erected in central public places for anyone who was literate in cuneiform to read.

On the other hand, the law codes were not completely divorced from actual judicial practice. There are some clear parallels and even convergence between the codes and law as carried out on a day-to-day basis. Some relationship apparently existed between the two spheres, but no explanation of the law codes has produced a consensus among experts in cuneiform jurisprudence. However, several suggestions seem to help clarification. The primary addressees of some of the codes are the gods. It was common for a king to deposit inscriptions (sometimes in the foundations of public buildings or temples) in which he asserted his loyalty, piety and wise kingship. Although these documents were intended primarily for the eyes of the gods, they might be circulated through public copies as well. The Codex Hammurabi has a lengthy prologue whose wording is similar to royal inscriptions known from foundation deposits. Hammurabi avers that he has honoured the gods, protected the weak, and otherwise promoted justice in his reign. The law itself, which was probably a revised compilation rather than a completely new entity, would be formal proof of the king's assertions.

Another suggestion about the origin of law codes—which does not necessarily conflict with the previous suggestion—is that they arose from scribal practice. It was the delight of scribes to organize, systematize, and catalogue. Many of the documents known from both Mesopotamia and Egypt consist of lists, daybooks, chronicles, and other attempts to organize knowledge (sometimes referred to as *Listenwissenschaft*, 'science of lists'). In some cases, practical necessity required that such material be available on file for reference, but other texts seem to have arisen from scribal views about order. It must be expected that scribes should, at some point, decide to make a formal compilation of legal practice. The first law codes were probably scribal compositions which had no immediate application. But when a king decided to issue some evidence of his wise and benevolent rule, it would have been a simple matter for the scribe to revise a pre-existing scribal composition to order, which the king could then promulgate as his new initiative.

In sum, the law codes were not legislation but compositions which probably arose for other reasons. The fact that they are by no means complete is a sign that they were not statute books. A great many areas of life are omitted, and no judge could have used them as a legal handbook. Yet the codes were based largely on standard legal process as it functioned in society at the time. There is a certain utopian quality about the codes, but they are more than just theory.

The situation in Israel seems to be similar. Some scholars have assumed that the Israelite codes functioned much as statute books in a modern state. For example, A. Phillips proposes that the ten commandments were the basis of criminal law in Israel, with violation of them a crime punishable by death. But this view seems to ignore the nature of the litera-

ture before us; although some sections of the Old Testament
are legal in nature, they are part of a religious document.
Within the Old Testament tradition itself, there are indications that society did not work according to the principles laid
down in the biblical text. A prime example of this is adultery.
According to Lev. 20.10, adultery was to be punished with
death. Elsewhere, however, the dangers of adultery (if
caught) are not said to be a public stoning but the wrath of an
irate husband who will not be appeased until he has done some
unpleasant things to the adulterer (Prov. 6.24-35). We have
little indication that adultery was ever an occasion for a public
trial and execution as the law envisaged.

As both B. Jackson and H. McKeating have pointed out,
many factors should be taken into account, including the
nature of the literature and statements elsewhere in the Old
Testament. As with the ancient Near Eastern law codes, the
laws in the Pentateuch probably bore some relation to actual
practices within society. They were not completely divorced
from how the society really worked, but they were not law
codes in a modern sense.

To conclude, there is a broad similarity in law over much of
the ancient Near East from Israel to Mesopotamia. Each
people selected, modified, refined, and developed the tradition
in its own way, but a significant overlap is easy to see in the
extant literature. Israel evidently drew on the common legal
and ethical tradition of its world, so that differences are generally of detail and emphasis rather than of conceptualization.
However, there is one major difference from the 'law codes'
known elsewhere in the ancient Near East: the Old
Testament mixes civic, religious, cultic, and ritual law in the
same texts. Since much of Leviticus is cultic material, this is
not generally paralleled in the legal texts of Mesopotamia and
elsewhere (though there may be parallels in ritual texts). It is
with Leviticus 19–20 that most legal comparisons can be
made.

Further Reading

On the dating of P, the following are important:

J. Blenkinsopp, 'The Structure of P', *CBQ* 38 (1976), pp. 275-92.

M. Haran, *Temples and Temple-Service in Ancient Israel* (Oxford: Clarendon Press, 1978).

A. Hurvitz, *A Linguistic Study of the Relationship between the Priestly Source and the Book of Ezekiel: A New Approach to an Old Problem* (Cahiers de la Revue Biblique 20; Paris: Gabalda, 1982).

—'Dating the Priestly Source in Light of the Historical Study of Biblical Hebrew: A Century after Wellhausen', *ZAW* 100 Supplement (1988), pp. 88-100.

Y. Kaufmann, *The Religion of Israel from its Beginnings to the Babylonian Exile* (trans. and abridged by M. Greenberg; London: George Allen & Unwin, 1961).

R. Polzin, *Late Biblical Hebrew: Toward an Historical Typology of Biblical Hebrew Prose* (HSM 12; Missoula, MT: Scholars Press, 1976).

J.G. Vink, 'The Date and Origin of the Priestly Code in the Old Testament', *OTS* 15 (1969), pp. 1-144.

M. Weinfeld, *Deuteronomy and the Deuteronomic School* (Oxford: Clarendon Press, 1972).

—*Deuteronomy 1-11* (AB; Garden City, NY: Doubleday, 1992).

J. Wellhausen, *Prolegomena to the History of Israel* (Edinburgh: A. & C. Black, 1885).

Z. Zevit, 'Converging Lines of Evidence Bearing on the Date of P', *ZAW* 94 (1982), pp. 481-511.

Those who have queried the existence of P, either as a separate document or the documentary hypothesis in general, include:

U. Cassuto, *The Documentary Hypothesis and the Composition of the Pentateuch* (Jerusalem: Magnes Press, 1961).

F. Cross, *Canaanite Myth and Hebrew Epic* (Cambridge, MA: Harvard University Press, 1973), pp. 293-95, 301-35.

R. Rendtorff, *The Problem of the Process of Transmission in the Pentateuch* (JSOTSup 89; Sheffield: JSOT Press, 1990).

R.N. Whybray, *The Making of the Pentateuch: A Methodological Study* (JSOTSup 53; Sheffield: JSOT Press, 1987).

On the origin and development of Israel as a nation, see especially the summary of scholarship in:

G.W. Ramsey, *The Quest for the Historical Israel* (Atlanta: John Knox, 1981).

See also some recent histories of Israel such as:

J.M. Miller and J.H. Hayes, *A History of Ancient Israel and Judah* (London: SCM Press, 1986).

On the cult or temple which may lie behind Leviticus (and P in general), see the following:

F.M. Cross, 'The Priestly Tabernacle', *BA* 10 (1947), pp. 45-68 (= *Biblical Archaeologist Reader*, I, pp. 201-28).

M. Haran, 'Shilo and Jerusalem: The Origin of the Priestly Tradition in the Pentateuch', *JBL* 81 (1962), pp. 14-24.

—*Temples and Temple-Service in Ancient Israel* (Oxford: Clarendon Press, 1978).

On the new methods and approaches, the following are helpful:

B.S. Childs, *Introduction to the Old Testament as Scripture* (Philadelphia: Fortress Press, 1979).

D. Damrosch, 'Leviticus', in *The Literary Guide to the Bible* (ed. R. Alter and F. Kermode; London: Collins, 1987), pp. 66-77.

R.P. Knierim, *Text and Concept in Leviticus 1.1-9: A Case in Exegetical Method* (Forschungen zum Alten Testament 2; Tübingen: Mohr [Paul Siebeck], 1992).

B.J. Schwartz, 'The Prohibitions concerning the "Eating" of Blood in Leviticus 17', in *Priesthood and Cult in Ancient Israel* (ed. G.A. Anderson and S.M.Olyan; JSOTSup 125; Sheffield: JSOT Press, 1991), pp. 34-66.

On ancient Near Eastern law and Old Testament law see:

H.J. Boecker, *Law and the Administration of Justice in the Old Testament and Ancient East* (Minneapolis: Augsburg, 1980).

S. Greengus, 'Law in the OT', *IDBSup* (1976), pp. 532-37.

B.S. Jackson, *Essays in Jewish and Comparative Legal History* (SJLA 10; Leiden: Brill, 1975), esp. pp. 25-63.

H. McKeating, 'Sanctions against Adultery in Ancient Israelite Society, with Some Reflections on Methodology in the Study of Old Testament Ethics', *JSOT* 11 (1979), pp. 57-72.

S. Paul, *Studies in the Book of the Covenant in the Light of Cuneiform and Biblical Law* (VTSup 18; Leiden: Brill, 1970).

D. Patrick, *Old Testament Law* (Atlanta: John Knox, 1985).

A. Phillips, *Ancient Israel's Criminal Law: A New Approach to the Decalogue* (Oxford: Blackwell, 1970).

R. Westbrook, 'Biblical and Cuneiform Law Codes', *RB* 92 (1985), pp. 247-64.

Many of the 'law codes' of the ancient Near East can be found translated in:

J.B. Pritchard (ed.), *Ancient Near Eastern Texts Relating to the Old Testament* (3rd edn with Supplement; Princeton: Princeton University Press, 1969).

On foundational deposits, see:

R.S. Ellis, *Foundation Deposits in Ancient Mesopotamia* (New Haven: Yale University Press, 1968).

2

THE SACRIFICIAL SYSTEM

THE MAIN SECTION DEVOTED to instructions about the types and methods of sacrifice is Leviticus 1–7, though other passages are concerned with the sacrificial system. As will be shown in more detail below, there is no unified system, as is clear from occasional contradictions and especially from the omissions and obscurity of vital information. There seems little doubt that a relationship exists between the material given and the actual cult in the temple during the monarchy, but it is difficult to be precise about its nature.

Main Types of Sacrifice in Leviticus

Leviticus 1–5 gives the basic instructions about the types of sacrifices to be offered. Much information seems to be presented with the ordinary Israelite who brings the sacrifice primarily in mind. Leviticus 6–7 is more directly concerned with the priests themselves. Having listed the main offerings in chs. 1–5, the compiler discusses the 'law' (*tôrāh*) of these offerings in chs. 6–7. There is a list of general instructions relating to all offerings or to certain ones specifically. These pertain more specifically to the priest(s) and may be part of inner-priestly lore. Thus, while chs. 6–7 seems to go over some of the same ground as chs. 1–5, the amount of real repetition is minimal.

A number of offerings are said to be *'iššeh*, which is often translated as 'offerings by fire'. This depends on the presumed origin of the word from *'ēš* 'fire', which is also reflected in later

translations. Such a translation presents two difficulties: some
offerings are referred to as '*iššeh* even when they are not
burned (the wine offering in Num. 15.10 for example),
whereas some offerings burned on the altar (the sin offering
for example) are not called '*iššeh*. Migrom has related the
word to Ugaritic *iṭṭ* 'gift' and perhaps Arabic '*aṭâṭu*
'possession of every kind'. He suggests the translation 'food
gift', perhaps a shortened term from *leḥem* '*iššeh,* 'food gift'
(Lev. 3.11, 16). In his opinion, the word may have become
obsolete by exilic times since it is absent from later Old
Testament collections.

The main term for offering is *qorbān*. This is a generic term
which refers to a variety of types. The instructions about how
to prepare the sacrifice are often stereotyped, so that similar
wording is used in the case of types which have parallel
features; however, it is interesting to notice that small differences in wording are often found even when the same
instructions seem to have been in mind. The schema for
animal sacrifices generally went as follows:

1. The sacrificer laid hands on the head of the animal.
2. It was killed at the entrance to the tabernacle, north of
    the altar, and cut up. It is often thought that this was
    done by the one making the offering rather than by
    the priest. If so, it contradicts Ezek. 44.11, where it is
    done by the Levites, and 2 Chron. 29.22-24, where it
    was done by the priests.
3. Blood was sprinkled, dashed or poured, usually on the
    sides and/or the base of the altar.
4. The parts burned in the case of cattle included the
    entrails with their fat, the kidneys and suet, and the
    caul of the liver; the same was true with sheep or
    goats, except that the fat tail was also added.
5. Except for the whole burnt offering, the breast of the
    animal went to the priests as a body, while the right
    thigh went to the presiding priest specifically.

In the case of birds the neck was wrung off but, rather than
being cut up, the body was torn open by the wings without
severing it.

For meal offerings the pattern was the following:

1. Choice flour was to be used, with oil mixed in before cooking or added afterwards; anything cooked was always unleavened; frankincense accompanied the offering.
2. The frankincense and a token portion of the flour or cake were burnt on the altar.
3. The rest of the offering went to the priest.

Burnt Offering ('ōlāh)

1.2-17; 6.1-6. Sometimes referred to as the 'holocaust', this whole burnt offering was the complete sacrifice, for none of it (except for the hide) went to the sacrificing priest or to the one making the offering. The entire animal was 'turned into smoke', to use the Hebrew expression (*hiqtîr*). The offering could be from the herd or flock, a male animal in either case, or from the birds (turtle doves or pigeons). Although the animal was cut up, all the pieces (not just the fat, kidneys, etc.) were placed on the altar. The legs and entrails were washed and then placed on the altar.

The burnt offering had an expiatory function, as is indicated by 1.4, 9.7, 14.20, and 16.24 (cf. also Ezek. 45.15, 17). But it seems to have been used for a wide range of other purposes, according to some passages at least, including entreaty (1 Sam. 13.12) and appeasement of God's wrath (1 Sam. 7.9; 2 Sam. 24.21-25). It could also be used as an occasion for rejoicing (Lev. 22.17-19; Num. 15.3). It has been suggested that because of its ubiquity in early texts, the whole burnt offering and the well-being offering (see below) were the only sacrifices in the earliest period, with the sin and guilt offerings being added later when the temple was established.

Cereal Offering (minḥāh)

2.1-16; 6.7-11. The meal offering followed the pattern outlined above. Raw flour could be used (mixed with oil) or the flour could be baked in an oven, cooked on a griddle, or fried in a pan. It was always unleavened since no leaven was to be burnt on the altar (2.11), and was to be salted (2.13) as a sign of the covenant. Other vegetable offerings could be brought: first-fruits (*rē'šit*)—no details given—or a cereal offering of first fruits (*bikkûrîm*) which was to consist of roasted grain with the usual oil and frankincense.

The word *minḥāh* means 'gift' and is used with a general meaning in some texts (in reference to animals in Gen. 4.3-4 and 1 Sam. 2.17) for example. It could even mean 'tribute' (Judg. 3.15; 2 Sam. 8.2). In Leviticus and priestly tradition in general, it refers exclusively to the offering of grain or meal. The cereal offering was the only non-blood sacrifice. It had two functions: (1) it was often an offering accompanying one of the others, in particular the burnt and thanksgiving offerings; (2) it could be offered in its own right as an independent sacrifice. The daily (*tāmîd*) offering seems to have included a cereal offering as well as a burnt offering in the morning (see below). At least one sacrifice (guilt offering) could consist of a cereal offering if the offerer's economic situation did not allow an animal. In the priestly tradition, only a token portion of the cereal offering was burnt on the altar in each case, and the rest went to the priest. Other texts indicate that this was an innovation, however, since it was apparently burnt entirely on the altar at one time (1 Kgs 8.64; 2 Kgs 16.13, 15). Even the wording of Lev. 6.10 suggests a change from a previous practice.

Sacrifice of Well-being (šĕlāmîm)
3.1-16; 7.11-18; 7.28-34. The precse connotation of the Hebrew *šĕlāmîm* in reference to this offering is uncertain, and different English renderings are found, depending on the supposed etymology of the word. It was long connected with *šālôm*, 'peace', and called the 'peace offering', a translation still found in the Revised Standard Version. Recent translations often derive the name from *šālēm* 'well-being', the translation used in the New Jewish Publication Society translation. Another idea is 'covenant' offering (perhaps connected with Akkadian *salīmu* 'covenant') as Levine has noted. However, there is no evidence that there was any connection between this offering and the covenant with God or that the

covenant was regularly celebrated with a sacrifice. Levine himself suggests the meaning 'gift', based on the Akkadian *šulmānu* which means 'gift of greeting'. The translation 'communion offering' has also been used, based on Robertson Smith's theory that this was the original function of the sacrifice (see below). As Milgrom notes, these are all only educated guesses, and exactly how the term is rendered is to some extent arbitrary.

Three sorts of sacrifice may be included under the 'well-being' offering:

1. The freewill offering (*nĕdāvāh*), given voluntarily on the part of the offerer, without any special motivation.
2. The votive offering (*nēder*). Whenever a vow was made, it was completed by an offering.
3. The thanksgiving offering (*tôdāh*), given as an expression of thanks for deliverance in time of trouble. There are several problems with understanding this offering. Is it the same as the freewill offering? Some scholars have thought so, while others (Milgrom for example) think the two are always clearly distinguished in the Old Testament and should be kept separate. There are certain anomalies about the *tôdāh* offering when compared with the other well-being offering which suggest that it was once considered separate. The main distinction from similar offerings is that it is accompanied by a cereal offering and must be eaten the same day it is offered. The freewill and votive offerings do not have the accompanying cereal offering and can be eaten either on the day of the offering or on the next day. Indeed, in other passages the thanksgiving offering does seem to be an independent offering alongside the well-being offering (Lev. 22.21, 29; Jer. 17.26; 2 Chron. 29.31-33; 33.16), and only in the supposed P source is it made a subdivision of the well-being offering.

The actual terminology used for the well-being offering is *zevaḥ šĕlāmîm* 'sacrifice of well-being'. The term *zevaḥ* is often translated by thre general term 'sacrifice'; however, it

seems to be limited to those sacrifices which were eaten by the
offerer, and would not be applied to the burnt offering or the
sin offering since these were burnt whole or eaten only by the
priests. The question is why the double terminology is used.
Rendtorff has suggested that two originally separate offerings
have been combined. Double terminology is unparalleled in
cultic texts. Also, *zevaḥ šelamim* is limited to Leviticus and
Numbers; *zevaḥ* often occurs by itself elsewhere, but *šelamim*
is never alone and is often used in the context of the burnt
offering. Milgrom, on the other hand, argues that *zevaḥ
šelamim* is merely a synonym for *šelamim*.

Sin Offering (ḥaṭṭā't)
4.1-35; 6.17-23. The term *ḥaṭṭā't* is traditionally translated
'sin offering' because the word also means 'sin'. The difficulty
with this translation is that the sacrifice is required in certain
cases where no sin is involved (Lev. 12.6 for example).
Therefore, Milgrom argues for the translation 'purificatory
offering'. His point is well taken; however, it seems a
cumbersome title and one which may not be readily apparent
to those more used to 'sin offering'. For this reason, 'sin
offering' is still used here despite this doubt.

The sin offering was to be made when a sin had been committed unwittingly. The instructions vary according to the
rank of the person offering it, and the pattern differs in
certain details from that already described. If the anointed
priest (apparently the high priest) was atoning for personal
sins, a bull was to be offered. The blood was sprinkled inside the
tabernacle itself, before the curtain covering the Holy of
Holies, and some of it was put on the horns of the incense altar.
The normal portions were burnt on the altar, but the rest of
the animal was taken outside the camp and burned in the
place where the ashes from the altar were disposed of. If the
whole community had sinned, the ceremony was the same
except that the elders took the part of the offerer.

If a tribal chieftain *(nāśî')* sinned, a male goat was offered,
and blood was put on the horns of the altar of burnt offerings.
In this case only the normal portions were burned, while the
rest went to the priest to be eaten. If an ordinary person ('*am*

hā'āreṣ) sinned, a female goat or sheep was offered; the other details were the same as for the chieftain.

It is clear that two sorts of sin offering are described here. One was offered because of the sin of the priests and was burnt entirely. The other, offered on behalf of the ordinary Israelite, was eaten by the priests after the normal parts were burned on the altar.

Guilt Offering ('āšām)

5.1-26; 7.1-10. The precise meaning of *'āšām* is not clear. The verb can mean 'to commit an offence' and 'to become guilty' (by committing an offence); hence the traditional translation 'guilt offering'. Milgrom opposes this translation, arguing that when it refers exclusively to cultic usage the term has four connotations: (1) reparation, (2) reparation offering, (3) the incurring of liability to someone, (4) the feeling of guilt. Milgrom emphasized this last example especially. The translation 'realize guilt' or 'become conscious of guilt', as found in a number of translations, he thinks is wrong. Rather, the clue to the sacrifice lies in the fact that the person became conscience-striken, afraid that an offence had been committed. For the offering itself, Milgrom uses the translation 'reparation offering'.

The breaches for which this was offered do not form a clear pattern since they include failing to act as a witness, uttering a rash oath, or touching the corpse of an unclean animal or some other unclean thing without realizing it. The person must first confess the sin, then bring an offering of a female goat or sheep which seems to have been treated like the sin offering. If the sinner could not afford a sheep or goat, it was permitted to bring two turtle doves or two pigeons, one for a burnt offering and one for a sin offering. Since there are no instructions about fowls for a sin offering, some details are given here: the neck was wrung but the head was not severed from the body, and part of the blood was sprinkled on the side of the altar while the rest was poured out at the base. What happened then is not stated. The flesh of the guilt offering normally went to the priest, after the fat and other selected pieces were burned on the altar, but there are no precise instructions about birds. The other bird is treated as a burnt offering. If the person did not have enough wealth for birds, a tenth of an *ephah* of fine flour (without oil or frankincense) was offered. A token portion was burnt, and the rest went to the priest, as was normal in cereal offerings.

Another sort of transgression involved unwitting violation of the 'holy things' of God (*qodšē yhwh*). The type of violation is not described, but the later ceremony suggests that the person used something belonging to God for his own purposes, for restitution had to be made, with another twenty per cent (fifth part) added to it (Lev. 5.16). A ram was brought, though its monetary equivalent was also allowed (Lev. 5.15; cf. Lev. 5.25 [Eng. 6.6]). The ram was, presumably, offered on the altar (cf. Lev. 5.16 with 5.6). These instructions are followed by a general statement that a ram was to be brought for any transgressions of Yahweh's commands which at first escaped the person's notice (5.17-19).

The concept is further expanded to include defrauding one's neighbour or robbery or not returning a lost object (5.20-26 [Eng. 6.1-7]). Again, restitution had to be made, with twenty per cent added, and a ram (or its equivalent value) was brought for a guilt offering.

The guilt offering was always a notorious problem, mainly because the precise distinction between guilt and sin offerings is not clear. Early Jewish commentators had difficulties in interpreting it (cf. Philo, *Spec. Leg.* 1.226-38; Josephus, *Ant.* 3.9.3 §230-32). The problem has also afflicted modern commentators, with various solutions being proposed. For example, Kellermann suggested that the guilt offering developed from the sin offering, providing a form of sacrifice between the sin and burnt offerings, as the atonement sacrifice for all cases of gross negligence. In Lev. 5.15, however, it is probably equivalent to the sin offering. Levine believes that it was not originally an altar sacrifice but a cultic offering presented to the deity in the form of silver or an object of value in expiation for certain offences. A necessary precondition was that the sin was inadvertent. Although Lev. 5.20-26 (Eng. 6.1-7) may seem to contradict this, because a false oath cannot be given inadvertently, Levine explains this as a separate category of crime.

Milgrom opposes Levine, taking the view that the guilt offering must be a blood sacrifice. Any mention of silver refers to buying an animal to sacrifice. As already indicated, Milgrom believes that the solution may be found in the meaning of the name, which he takes to mean 'feel guilt' when there is no verbal object. The notion common to all offences which call for the guilt sacrifice is that they are all cases of sacrilege against God, either by an infringement of holy things or by a trespass against the name of God.

Daily Offering (tāmîd)

One offering was for the priests specifically. This was the daily meal offering described in Lev. 6.12-16, offered on behalf of Aaron and his sons. It consisted of a tenth of an *ephah* of fine flour (about 2 litres), mixed with oil, and cooked on a griddle. Half was offered in the morning and half in the evening. This was burned entirely on the altar, with no portion eaten by the priests.

The daily offering was extremely important in antiquity because it was the main sign that the temple was functioning and that God was accessible to the people. When the daily sacrifice was stopped, it indicated times of dire consequences, as when the temple was destroyed by Nebuchadnezzar or the Romans, or when the sacrifice was stopped by force in the time of the Maccabees. Surprisingly perhaps, what constituted the daily offering is not clear. Leviticus mentions only the cereal offering of the high priest, made in the morning and evening. Other priestly passages mention a daily burnt offering of two lambs, one in the morning and one in the evening (Exod. 29.38-42; Num. 28.3-8). Was this separate from the cereal offering or was the cereal offering thought of only as a companion offering? (Note that the cereal offering of Exodus and Numbers is two tenths of an *ephah*, but only one tenth in Lev. 6.13.) If the cereal offering accompanied it, why is this not mentioned in Leviticus, and why is the required drink offering also ignored?

Other passages are different again. In the time of the Maccabees, the practice of sacrificing the *tāmîd* twice a day is day is attested in Dan. 8.11-14, while 9.21 mentions an evening cereal offering. 2 Kgs 16.15 refers to a morning burnt offering and an evening cereal offering (cf. also 1 Sam. 18.29, 36). Ezek. 46.13-15 differs from Exodus, Leviticus, and Numbers in describing a daily sacrifice of one lamb (not two), accompanied by a sixth of an *ephah* of flour (instead of a tenth). This illustrates the difficulty of ascertaining actual practice from the biblical texts alone, with no other literature extant.

Priestly Dues

One of the special concerns of Leviticus 6–7 is that of the sacrificial portions which go to the priests. Some offerings (such as the burnt offering) were burned entirely, but for most only certain parts of the animal went on the altar while the rest was either divided between the offerer and the offering priest or went entirely to the priest. On priestly dues in general, see ch. 4.

Interpreting the Israelite Sacrificial System

No complete system of sacrifice is expounded in Leviticus. This is clear from other references and hints within the Old Testament literature and a comparison with other cultic systems. For example, there is no treatment of drink offerings as such, although they are mentioned several times as an essential accompaniment to some of the blood sacrifices. The exact function of the cereal offerings in the system is problematic. Salt is only mentioned specifically with the cereal offerings, yet it was evidently required to be used with all offerings (Lev. 2.13). The incompleteness of the information generally is also indicated by apparent contradictions between various passages. In sum, this is not a priestly handbook to be memorized by the novice and consulted by the practising priests.

Nevertheless, even though the complete sacrificial system cannot be fully understood on the basis of this text, some important issues need to be addressed.

Order of Sacrifice

At several points in Leviticus and elsewhere there is a command to bring more than one offering. However, those in Leviticus 8–9 are listed in a different sequence from those in Numbers 7 and 28–29. Also, the Nazarite brings sacrifices in the order of burnt offering, sin offering, well-being offering, cereal offering, and drink offering, but the sequence of actual sacrifice is different, the burnt and sin offerings changing place. A. Rainey, following on from Levine, argued that one text represents procedure whereas the other is scribal description. In his opinion, the sin (or guilt) offering came first because sin had to be dealt with before anything else. Next came the closely related burnt offering, and only then the accompanying cereal and drink offerings. Levine took a different position, arguing that the burnt offering came first because it served to invoke God, after which the sin offering would be effective. Milgrom agrees with Rainey on the grounds that the sin offering must come first in order to purge the sanctuary of any impurities, while the burnt offering is a type of gift to God.

The problem with these discussions is that they too often interpret the text on the basis of presumed logic. What might seem logical to us, however, is not necessarily how things were perceived when the cult was in actual operation. That a sin offering must come first may seem logical to a modern Westerner, but did the ancient Israelite priests think the same way? Or does the problem lie with the tradition, which only partially corresponded with actual cult practice and which, in any case, is incomplete?

Forgiveness of Sins

Not all offerings were for sins, of course, and such matters as ritual pollution, childbirth, thanksgiving, and vows were an important part of the system even though they were not connected with sin. Yet it is also true that sin is central to some sacrifices (the sin offering for example), and several passages state that the offerers will have their sins forgiven (Lev. 4.20, 26, 31, 35; 5.10, 13, 16, 18).

The question remains: how does the forgiveness operate?

What does the offering purify? The expected answer is 'The person who committed the sin'. But why is the blood sprinkled on the altar and not on the person? Milgrom argues that it did not serve to purify the one who had committed a cultic breach (because washing and the going down of the sun purify) or sinned (because such was not required). Instead, he maintains that sin and pollution were 'an aerial miasma that possessed magnetic attraction for the realm of the sacred'. In other words, sin affected the sanctuary, which had to be purged by the sin offering. There were three sorts of pollution: (1) the physical impurity or inadvertent misdemeanour of an ordinary Israelite, which polluted the temple court; (2) the same for a priest or the entire community, which polluted the tabernacle itself; (3) wanton unrepented sin, which polluted even the Holy of Holies.

There is no question that sin affected the altar and sanctuary and had to be atoned for (Exod. 30.10; Lev. 16.16-19; Ezek. 43.19-26). What is less certain is that the offering had no bearing on the forgiveness of the offerer's sins. Such an idea seems to go against the context and common sense. If the person was forgiven after the sacrifice, surely the sacrifice must have been in some way involved. The problem may be one of conceptualization. To use Milgrom's argument, would the blood have to be sprinkled on the offerer to cleanse the sin? Cultic logic does not necessarily work as one might anticipate. If the victim is somehow identified with the offerer, acting as a sort of surrogate or substitute, the shedding of the animal's blood and the loss of its life could be the essential aspect of the ritual which removed the sin. As the Nuer say about one of their own sacrifices (Evans-Pritchard), it may be 'that what they [the Israelites, in this case] are doing is to place all evil in their hearts on to the back of the beast and that it then flows into the earth with the...blood'. This brings us to the question of the significant term *kipper*.

Meaning of kipper
The word *kipper* is used in a number of contexts to describe the removal of sin or ritual impurity. Although often trans-lated as 'atone' or 'cover up', its precise connotation has been

much debated. Levine has argued that it means 'remove, wipe off' impurity, not 'cover up'. The denominative verb means 'serve as a ransom, expiation gift'. In the cult, the word was used primarily in functional terms to mean 'perform rites of expiation' rather than 'cleanse'. Milgrom sees a development in the word from a basic meaning 'purge'. It also carried the idea of 'rub, wipe', so that the meanings 'cover' (that is, 'wipe on') and 'wipe off' are complementary rather than contradictory. In ritual texts, the idea of 'wipe off' predominated in that the blood was thought of as wiping off impurity, acting as a sort of cultic detergent. With certain rituals, such as those on the Day of Atonement or involving the red cow (Num. 19.1-10), the idea of 'ransom' or 'substitute' was the main connotation. This finally led to the meaning 'atone, expiate' in some passages, especially with regard to all sacrifices where blood was not daubed on the horns of the altar.

There is, however, a major disagreement between Milgrom and Levine about the function of the blood. Levine argues that it has two functions: (1) an apotropaic function for the deity; that is, the blood was placed on the altar to protect God from the malignancy of impurity which was regarded as an external force; (2) a purificatory or expiatory role, in which the blood served as a ransom substituting for the life owed by the offerer.

According to Milgrom, the idea of demonic or malignant forces which might harm the deity had no place in the thought of the P tradition. Impurities did compromise the holiness of the sanctuary and altar, so the purpose of the offering was to remove these. As noted above, his opinion is that the blood acted as a ritual detergent, washing off the impurities which had attached themselves to the sacred things. The question of demonic forces is really a separate issue and will not be taken up here. More important is what is thought to have happened when an animal was slain at the altar. Milgrom dismisses the idea of the sacrificial victim as a substitute for the sinner. He does acknowledge, though, that on the 'day of *kippurîm*' (*yôm hakkippurîm* or Day of Atonement) the sins were placed metaphorically on the head of the goat for Azazel. In this case, there is no sense of 'wiping off' but rather of the transfer of sins from the people to the animal.

That this ceremony really represents a type of substitute or surrogate for the sinner is a point well made by Kiuchi who specifically interacts with and criticizes Milgrom on this point. Kiuchi argues that the sin offering is envisaged as a substitute for the sinner, and that it purges the sin of the individual, not only the pollution of the sanctuary. The transfer of sins in the Day of Atonement ceremony may be different from this, since the victim is sent away and not slain. Nevertheless, he argues that the scapegoat ceremony is a form of sin offering.

This transfer of sins might be indicated when the offerer lays his hands on the animal's head. Kiuchi notes that there are several interpretations of this act. Although he favours the interpretation that it represents substitution, he recognizes that the evidence is scanty. Knierim opposes the idea of substitution and considers the gesture (which he translates as 'firm pressing down of the hand') to be a means of denoting transfer of ownership, that is, from the offerer to God. If so, this aspect of the discussion does not resolve the main problem of the elimination of sin.

Perhaps part of the problem is the consequence of being too literal in interpretation. The sacrificial system was a symbolic system, filled with metaphor, allegory, and analogy. It would be a mistake to assume that only one symbol or metaphor was used for removing sin (ritual detergent, for example). In the same way, the cultic terminology may have a more general meaning and should not be defined simply in terms of the specific metaphor used. The individual's sin was removed, whatever the precise symbolic conceptualization used.

Repentance

The sacrificial system has been widely accepted as a theological accounting system in which sin is 'paid for' by offering a life. Such a mechanistic view has, of course, been the object of considerable Christian polemic. Where is the place of the heart in all this? It has been thought that the prophets were those who first introduced the idea of repentance and inward change and hence a dismissal of the cult. Recent scholarship considers this to be simplistic. The prophets, whatever their criticisms of the cult, did not generally intend the end of all sacrifices. Rather, they polemicized against a variety of matters, including unlawful cultic practices, non-Yahwistic worship, and allowing form to stand for substance.

Yet the prophetic critique was not the first recognition that there was more to removing sin than cutting an animal's throat. Milgrom made the point that the concept of repentance and change of heart is already explicit within the cultic regulations of Leviticus. For example, there are five cases of deliberate sin which require a sacrifice, and all five also require confession. The priestly innovation, in Milgrom's opinion, is that confession did not erase the sin but reduced a deliberate crime to one done inadvertently. Although this concept did not reach the pinnacle of prophetic teaching, in which repentance could bring complete remission of sin, it was on the road towards that outcome.

More important is another problem: priests had to be particularly concerned about correct cultic procedure. To list technical details about how to carry out sacrifice in the right way was necessary and probably explains Leviticus in part. However, that reveals nothing about the meaning given by those same priests to the ritual they were carrying out with such exactitude. All ritual and liturgy has meaning, however repetitive and mechanical it may seem on the surface. What is apparent—at least, to some extent—are the mechanics of sacrifice; what is lacking is the theology which accompanied it. This fact has often been overlooked and has led scholars to dismiss the priestly material as dead ritual rather than living spirit.

Towards a General Theory of Sacrifice

The idea of sacrifice seems to be ubiquitous among human societies the world over. Even those that have abandoned it in their contemporary forms of worship, especially in more developed countries, have sacrifice as a part of their past. Since the concept goes so far back in human history that its origins are no longer traceable, we are left only with hypothesis and speculation as to how sacrifice came to be a part of the religious culture of most peoples. In a recent publication, edited by R.G. Hamerton-Kelly, some influential ideas are discussed between R. Gerard, W. Burkert, and J.Z. Smith, with others participating. Both Gerard and Burkert propose theories of the origin of sacrifice.

Considerably influenced by Freud, Gerard has argued that violence is endemic to human nature. Sacrifice originated in a primal collective murder. Since murder begets murder, the act is mythologized and rationalized by the use of a surrogate, an innocent victim. An arbitrary act is given meaning and the rivalries within the community covered over by a fictional interpretation of this act. Burkert has proposed that the notion of sacrifice goes back to Palaeolithic man the hunter, with the sacrifice being a ritualized form of the hunt and kill. The insights of both these theories have been recognized but they also raise problems. For one thing, sacrifice consists of domestic animals, not wild ones, certainly in the overwhelming number of instances. As Smith notes, the first point of sacrifice is its domesticity, not its 'primitiveness'. Secondly, anthropologists are generally uneasy about psychological theories which are not based on actual field study (like Freud, Gerard depends primarily on literature) and have not been happy with Gerard's explanation (see de Heusch; also Resaldo [in Hamerton-Kelly]). A third problem is that most of the evidence is recent, and it is not possible to reach back with any confidence to Palaeolithic times.

The precise origin of sacrifice is probably less important for the understanding of the system in Leviticus than the question of the function or conceptualization of sacrifice. A number of theories have been advanced in the past, some now long abandoned by anthropologists. Some of the most helpful include the following.

1. *Gift*. Proposed by the pioneering anthropologist E.B. Tylor, the thought was that humans have a natural desire to establish a union with the supernatural. The gift might serve to appease the wrath of a god or to evoke good will towards the offerer or to do both. The idea of a gift to the deity—if not necessarily a disinterested present—is found behind a number of sacrifices. Evans-Pritchard has identified this for many of

the Nuer sacrifices. It fits some of the Israelite sacrifices, at least in part, but it is not a universal explanation since there is much about sacrifice which it does not explain.

2. *Communion with God.* William Robertson Smith, a scholar who applied the new anthropological science to the Old Testament, argued that in sacrifice the community was eating a meal with their deity. His theory was tied up with the concept of totemism which was dominant at the time. He thought that the idea of a totemic animal which represented the divine was basic to all early human groups. When they slaughtered a totem animal, they were in some sense consuming their god and thus establishing communion with him. J.G. Frazer and others attempted to build on this; however, more recent scholarship has shown that totemism is limited to only a few tribes, and many sacrifices are not seen as a meal with God. For example, burnt offerings could hardly be a communal meal since they are entirely burned on the altar. Among the Nuer, the meat of the sacrifice is consumed, but only in a secular context after the sacrificial rites are complete. Nevertheless, Robertson Smith's basic idea of a communion meal explains certain types of sacrifice, such as the Israelite offering of well-being.

3. *Substitution.* The idea here is that the victim takes the place of, or in some way represents, the offerer. Such an explanation of sacrifice is widespread. As Evans-Pritchard noted, if one had to sum up Nuer sacrifice in one word, it would be 'substitution', life for life. This idea is central, even though, as he goes on to comment, such a summary does not do full justice to the complexity of the situation. Whether or not Evans-Pritchard is correct about the Nuer (see the criticisms of de Heusch), the idea of substitution seems present in some sacrifices. As noted in the previous section, this concept is controversial for Israelite sacrifice, but it seems that a good case can be made for this concept behind such offerings as the sin offering.

4. *Rite of passage.* As van Gennep recognized almost a century ago, at central points in the life cycle (puberty, marriage, funerals) there may be rites which assist the social and psychological transfer from one state to another.

Typically, these include (1) rites of separation; (2) transition rites; (3) rites of incorporation. The rite of separation removes the person from the old state and cuts off any binding ties. There is a necessary transitional phrase, a liminal state, which may even be dangerous. The final part of the rite is the welcome to and accommodation of the person into the new state or sphere. Not every one of the three stages is present in all cases, and one or two may be emphasized at the expense of the other(s).

A rite of separation is especially important in some sacrifices where the purpose of the sacrifice is to separate the offerer from something considered alien (de Heusch). For example, far from wanting to identify with the supernatural, in some cases the desire is to make a separation, to remove the supernatural from the sphere of the mundane where it is creating problems. The sacred can be dangerous, especially if it is operating where it is not wanted and where the unwary may unwittingly may encroach upon it.

It has been suggested that some sacrifices can be characterized as rites of passage. Certainly, ceremonies of initiation are typically rites of passage (the consecration of Aaron and his sons to the priesthood, for example). A. Marx has argued that the sin offering also functions as a rite of separation, while the burnt offering serves to reintegrate the person back into the cultic community. Milgrom opposes this, partly on the ground of the presumed order of the sacrifices and partly because of his view that the sin offering purges the altar, not the sinner. Nevertheless, the idea should be explored further.

Above all, however, central to sacrifice are the notions of expiation, cleansing, and re-establishment of cosmic—or at least microcosmic—harmony. If evil could not be removed, sin wiped away, pollution purified, and harmony restored, there would be little point in sacrifice. Therefore, regardless of the precise terms in which sacrifices were conceived (substitution, ritual detergent, scapegoat), the desired outcome is clear. In the scapegoat form of ceremony, sins and the like were heaped onto the head of the victim which was then separated from the community. In other cases, the victim was identified with the offerer even if precise identification was not required.

The laying of the hands on the victim by the offerer in Israelite sacrifice may have had a function along these lines. Regardless of the rite, the desire was to cause the sins, pollutions, illness, or troubles to vanish.

Further Reading

In addition to the commentaries listed in Chapter 1, there are several general treatments of the sacrificial system in ancient Israel, plus some detailed studies:

G.A. Anderson, *Sacrifices and Offerings in Ancient Israel: Studies in their Social and Political Importance* (HSM 41; Atlanta: Scholars Press, 1987).

N. Kiuchi, *The Purification Offering in the Priestly Literature: Its Meaning and Function* (JSOTSup 56; Sheffield: JSOT Press, 1987).

B.A. Levine, *In the Presence of the Lord: A Study of Cult and Some Cultic Terms in Ancient Israel* (SJLA 5; Leiden: Brill, 1974).

J. Milgrom, *Cult and Conscience: The ASHAM and the Priestly Doctrine of Repentance* (Leiden: Brill, 1976).

A.F. Rainey, 'The Order of Sacrifices in Old Testament Ritual Texts', *Bib* 1 (1970), pp. 485-98.

R. Rendtorff, *Studien zur Geschichte des Opfers im alten Israel* (WMANT 24; Neukirchen–Vluyn: Neukirchener Verlag, 1967).

R.J. Thompson, *Penitence and Sacrifice in Early Israel outside the Levitical Law: An Examination of the Fellowship Theory of Early Israelite Sacrifice* (Leiden: Brill, 1963).

R. de Vaux, *Ancient Israel* (2 vols.; London: Darton, Longman & Todd, 1961).

—*Studies in Old Testament Sacrifice* (Cardiff: University of Wales Press, 1964).

D.P. Wright, *The Disposal of Impurity: Elimination Rites in the Bible and in Hittite and Mesopotamian Literature* (SBL Dissertation Series 101; Atlanta: Scholars Press, 1987).

In addition to these, entries on individual sacrifices can be found in the *Theological Dictionary of the Old Testament (Theologisches Wörterbuch des Alten Testaments)*, including D. Kellerman on the *asham*, and in the *Theologisches Handwörterbuch des Alten Testaments*.

On the anthropological questions about the origins and general theory of sacrifice, see the following:

M.F.C. Bourdillon and M. Fortes (eds.), *Sacrifice* (London: Academic Press, 1980). See especially the introductory articles by the editors and articles by J.H.M. Beattie and J.W. Rogerson.

E. Evans-Pritchard, *Nuer Religion* (Oxford: Oxford University Press, 1956).

A. van Gennep, *The Rites of Passage* (London: Routledge & Kegan Paul, 1960).

L. de Heusch, *Sacrifice in Africa: A Structuralist Approach* (Manchester: Manchester University Press, 1985). Note his criticisms of Evans-Pritchard, pp. 6-14, and Gerard, pp. 16-17.

R.G. Hamerton-Kelly (ed.), *Violent Origins: Ritual Killing and Cultural Formation* (Stanford, CA: Stanford University Press, 1987).

A. Marx, 'Sacrifice pour les péchés ou rites de passage? Quelques réflexions sur la fonction *du ḥaṭṭā't'*, *RB* 96 (1989), pp. 27-48.

W. Robertson Smith, *Lectures on the Religion of the Semites: The Foundational Institutions* (ed. S. Cook; London: A. & C. Black, 3rd edn, 1927).

E.B. Tylor, *Primitive Culture: Researches into the Development of Mythology, Philosophy, Religion, Language, Art, and Custom* (2 vols.; New York: John Murray, 5th edn, 1913).

3

CLEAN AND UNCLEAN, PURITY AND POLLUTION

ONE OF THE BASIC CONCEPTS of Israelite society, as it relates to religion and the cult, is that of cultic purity and pollution. 'Clean' (*ṭāhôr*) and 'unclean' (*ṭāmē'*) were important images. At the most basic level, to be clean allowed one to participate in the cult, whereas those who were unclean were excluded. Yet there is also the impression that uncleanness needed to be removed even when access to the cult was unlikely in the near future. It was no sin to become unclean, but one should not remain in a state of impurity.

A common misconception is that these matters were concerned with hygiene—that unclean meant 'dirty'; such is not the case. Granted, many things said to be unclean might be dirty from the present-day point of view, but not necessarily all. In any event, one did not become clean simply with a little soap and water. Washing was often required but was not sufficient in itself; the going down of the sun or a longer passage of time might be necessary before cultic cleanness was restored.

The main section in Leviticus which deals with purity is chs. 11–15 but many other verses which presuppose the concept or discuss it are found scattered throughout the book.

The Leviticus Account

Leviticus 11. Animal Food
Eating was a central aspect of purity. Certain things were not to be eaten. The Israelite was to be concerned about the types

of animal considered fit for consumption and how they were to be prepared. Leviticus 11 (paralleled by Deuteronomy 14) lists the various animals available for food and those to be avoided. There are some difficulties here because it is not always clear which animals are being referred to. Especially problematic are the various birds of vv. 13-19.

The mammals and sea life are fairly easy to differentiate. For mammals (vv. 2-8) two questions are asked: Does it chew the cud? Does it have cloven hooves? If the response to both these questions is 'yes', the animal can be eaten; if 'no' to either or both, it is forbidden. Borderline cases are mentioned to clarify the matter: The pig has cloven hooves but does not chew the cud; the camel chews the cud but does not have cloven hooves; the hare might be thought to chew the cud, because of the movements of its jaws, but it has no hooves. In scientific terminology, mammal food is limited to the ruminating bi-hooved members of the order *Artiodactyla*.

The eating of sea creatures is restricted to those which have fins and scales (vv. 9-12). No animals are named, but it is clear that some fish (those without scales), all crustaceans, and most other fresh- and saltwater animals are forbidden.

The distinctions between birds are hard to ascertain because not all can be positively identified (vv. 13-19). Nevertheless, the majority of those which can be recognized are carnivores or scavengers. Other flying things are also discussed here, including the bat (unclean) and some insects. A few insects could be eaten, mainly of the locust, cricket, or grasshopper type (vv. 20-23).

After this the account seems to repeat itself, with quadrupeds again (vv. 24-28), followed by a long section on 'swarming things' (vv. 29-45). However, some structure does emerge on closer examination, since vv. 24-40 are primarily concerned with the carcasses of unclean animals, not with the animals themselves. Then, vv. 41-45 are about the swarming things which had not been discussed fully in vv. 1-23. Despite a more or less coherent structure, most critics see evidence here of development and supplementation. Further evidence of this is found in vv. 43-45 which use language reminiscent of H: 'be holy as I am holy'.

Leviticus 12. Woman after Childbirth
The first form of impurity for women listed in Leviticus is that of childbirth. If a woman bore a boy, she was unclean for seven days, until the circumcision of the boy on the eighth day. For another thirty-three days she was not strictly unclean (that is, passing on uncleanness to others who had contact with her) but was not allowed to come into the sanctuary or touch any holy thing. These periods were doubled for the birth of a girl to fourteen and sixty-six days. The allotted period was completed and purity restored with a lamb for a burnt offering and a pigeon or dove for a sin offering. A poor person could substitute two pigeons or doves, one for the burnt offering and one for the sin offering.

Leviticus 13–14. 'Leprosy'
These chapters deal with a disease which has traditionally been translated 'leprosy', but modern scholars are almost universal in rejecting this as the appropriate term. The Hebrew term ṣāra'at clearly covers a variety of scaly skin diseases, as well as types of mildew in houses or garments. The modern condition known as leprosy is limited to Hanson's disease. By contrast, it is not clear that modern leprosy is even covered by the ancient disease: there is some question whether Hanson's disease was known in the Mediterranean world before the Hellenistic period.

The main function of the priest in this connection was to examine any affliction or inflammation, to isolate the individual if it looked like the real disease, to check again after seven days, and finally to pronounce the afflicted person whole or leprous. Despite the length of the regulations, they are fairly repetitive, with slightly different criteria for scale patches, burns, boils, and so on.

Most commentators recognize that the text is not concerned with medical treatment or hygiene but rather with ritual. What is being discussed is not how to treat the various diseases under the rubric ṣara'at but only how to recognize them and how to view them from the point of view of cultic purity. The medical question was no doubt important in Israel but it is not within the scope of the discussion here. The job of the priest was to pronounce on ritual purity and impurity, and the text gives some guidance on how to decide whether the person is clean or not. The disease as such was not being treated. Even the isolation was not a quarantine for purposes of preventing the spread of the disease but only a way of allowing it time to develop or recede so that an authoritative pronouncement could be made about it.

The identification of the disease(s) falling under the generic term ṣara'at is further complicated by the fact that some conditions of cloth and skin (Lev. 13.47-59) and of houses (Lev. 14.33-53) are also included. These sections appear to deal with mould or fungus infections. From a medical point of view there is no connection between these and the aforementioned skin diseases. This reinforces the view that something other than pathological conditions is in the mind of the writer.

A good deal of space is devoted to the question of re-entry into the cultic community once the disease is cured (Lev. 14.1-32). A major feature was a ritual in which two birds were taken, one killed but the other released into the open country. This ritual obviously had certain features in common with the scapegoat ritual (Leviticus 16), especially with the use of two creatures, one of which is killed and the other released. The person healed then had to wash body and clothes, shave off all hair, and remain outside the tent (though within the camp) for a further seven days. The healed person then presented three lambs (one for a guilt offering, one for a sin offering, and one for a burnt offering), a cereal offering, and a quantity of oil. Some of the blood of the guilt offering and some of the oil were put on different parts of the former sufferer's body. A poor person need bring only one lamb (for the guilt offering), two turtle doves or pigeons (for the sin and burnt offerings), the cereal offering, and the oil.

It was also envisaged that a house could contract ṣara'at (Lev. 14.33-53). Such a house would be isolated for seven days, just like a person. If the area of 'infection' had grown, the stones of the affected area were replaced and the walls scraped and replastered. If it broke out and spread after this, the house would be demolished. If not, it would be pronounced clean. The cleansing would be completed with the ceremony of the two birds, as with a person.

Likewise, the infected object could be a piece of cloth or leather (13.47-59). This would be isolated for seven days. If the condition had spread during that time, it was pronounced unclean and burned. If not, it was to be washed, then isolated for another seven days. If the contamination had entirely disappeared, it would be washed a second time and pronounced clean. If it had faded but not disappeared, the affected area was torn out and the garment would be pronounced unclean only if there was a recurrence. If the washing did not remove or fade the infection, it was pronounced unclean and burned.

Leviticus 15. Genital Discharges

This chapter deals with a variety of genital discharges, normal and abnormal, for both men and women. The first to be treated were men (vv. 2-18). If there was an abnormal emission of semen or other penile discharge, the man (*zāv*) became impure. The pollution was passed on to anyone touching him or anything on which he sat; also, if he spat on anyone or touched anyone without first washing his hands. The person so polluted was required to bathe in spring water and wash his clothes, after which he would become clean with the going down of the sun.

A normal discharge of semen in marital intercourse (Lev. 15.16-18) was also polluting, though less contagious than an abnormal discharge. Both the man and the woman were to wash themselves and remain unclean until evening. Any cloth or leather object on which semen fell was also to be washed and to remain unclean until evening.

With regard to women, the flow of blood caused by childbirth was dealt with in Lev. 12.1-8. The most basic regular genital discharge was the monthly period (Lev. 15.19-24). The period of impurity lasted seven days even if the actual flow of blood finished sooner. During this time the woman transmitted impurity by direct context, or indirectly through anything on which she sat or lay. All who touched her or that on which she lay or sat would need to wash themselves and their clothes and be unclean until evening. A man who had sexual relations with her would be unclean for seven days.

All these discharges were regarded as more or less 'normal'
because the person who became polluted by them would be
purified by washing and the passage of time. There was no
requirement to offer a sacrifice.

Any other prolonged discharge of blood in the case of a
woman also brought on uncleanness of the same order as
menstruation (Lev. 15.25-30). If the flow stopped, the woman
would become clean after seven days. In this case, though,
there was a significant difference, for she had to make a
sacrifice. On the eighth day she was to bring two pigeons or
doves, one for a burnt offering and one for a sin offering.

Rationale for the Purity Laws

The purity and pollution rules in Judaism have often been
discussed over the centuries. Many have dismissed them as
primitive superstition or evidence of an antiquated legal
mentality. The Jews themselves, while regarding the regulations as essential, have been as puzzled as others. The *Letter of
Aristeas* (third–second century BCE) attempted to explain that
certain animals were forbidden for food in order to teach
moral qualities (*Letter of Aristeas* 142–51). Even in antiquity
it was argued that the rules were purely arbitrary, designed
by God simply to teach discipline to the Jews and to set them
apart (cf. *Sifra*, Qedoshim 11.22). Such a view also finds favour
among some modern scholars. More recently still, it has been
common to clarify these rules in terms of hygiene: shell fish
were not eaten because they go off quickly in a hot climate; one
can get trichinosis from pork; the washings and the like were
simply for bodily cleanliness; shutting up the potential leper
was a form of quarantine; and so on. As we shall see, some of
these suggestions have more merit than others.

With regard to the various sorts of impurity dealt with in
Leviticus 12–15 (flows of blood, other bodily discharges and
scaly diseases) Milgrom has put forward a cogent argument
for seeing life versus death as the common element. Blood,
according to Lev. 17.11, 14, contains life within itself.
Therefore, any loss of blood can be considered life-threatening.
Similarly, semen is associated with life, and its discharge is

suggestive of the loss of life-essence. Various skin diseases give the afflicted person the appearance of death, as do the mould/fungal infestations which may affect cloth or buildings. Thus, life is the central factor; and those aspects of life which suggest death are causes of impurity. This would also explain why dung is not considered impure in the Israelite system, since it is the normal product of the life processes and has no special association with death.

More problematic is Milgrom's position on the reason for the laws of Leviticus 11 about which animals may be eaten. He argues that their primary function was to teach the importance of, and respect for, animal life. The laws of Leviticus 11 and other passages on this subject mean that the use of meat from animals was extremely restricted. Also, the requirement that all slaughter must take place at the altar added a further restriction. Thus, according to Milgrom, even though meat was allowed, the occasions and amount of consumption were necessarily diminished. The only area where an Israelite might 'indulge' was with the hunting of wild game, although here again the species allowed to be eaten were limited.

Whatever the cogency of this explanation, any theory about the purity system in Israel must take account of recent anthropological study of the question.

Insights from Anthropology

One of the important discoveries of anthropology in the past fifty years is that purity and pollution systems are not arcane, primitive superstition. The precise form of the rituals may be arbitrary, at least to some extent, but recent study suggests that broader concerns are at the heart of any purity system. Purity and pollution form an important mirror of the society itself, especially its social relations and attitudes. They map the ideological cosmos of the people who hold these views. The various regulations may be seen as a language, in the broad sense of the term, communicating to those within the society the 'correct' attitudes towards relations between the sexes, marriage, kinship, and intercourse with outsiders. Ritual cleanliness shows the people how to classify the entities—human and animal—which inhabit the world around them, and communicates to the society in question how new forms which enter its world should be fitted in. The animal world and the way it is treated also maps human society; and the human community is represented by the body of the individual.

Clean and Unclean Animals

One of the major attempts to work out the meaning of the biblical system in detail was Mary Douglas's seminal book *Purity and Danger*, which has a chapter on the 'abominations of Leviticus'. 'Order' was the key. She argued that food taboos were a way of trying to impose order on an untidy existence. Certain animals were forbidden for food because they did not fit major categories of the Israelite classification system for animals, cutting across more than one class of animal, and were thus anomalous according to the cosmos of the Israelites. For this system Douglas relied primarily on Genesis 1, as well as Leviticus 11 (and Deuteronomy 14). The three spheres inhabited by animals are sea, air, and land, thus giving a tripartite classification system. For each sort, there was an appropriate system of locomotion (swimming with fins and scales in the sea or, in the case of flying creatures, using two wings and two legs). Certain creatures, however, did not fit into these three categories (the 'swarming things', for example) or did not have the form of locomotion appropriate to their class—for example, some creatures which have 'hands' instead of forefeet.

Although this explanation made a good deal of sense from many angles, there remained difficulties which would be as obvious to most Old Testament scholars as to anthropologists who criticized aspects of Douglas's book. One weakness is that judgments were made on the basis of English translations of the book; inability to consult the Hebrew text led her astray in some cases. A good example of this is the argument that some creatures were forbidden because they had 'hands'. In fact, the Hebrew word *kaf* refers to the 'palms' of the hands or 'soles' of the feet and has nothing to do with being shaped like a human hand. She also failed to note that those creatures which had 'palms' were not in the category of 'creeping things', contrary to the basis of her own argument.

Douglas took up the question again at several points in *Implicit Meanings*, especially in the last chapter, in order to clarify various points and take the issue further. Still not satisfactorily resolved was her continued insistence that the animals forbidden were anomalous from a classificatory point of view. This is strange since *most* animals, not just a few, were forbidden. There is nothing anomalous, for example, about the locomotion of the pig, camel, or many other forbidden animals. It is not plausible that only a few animals fell inside the classification system and that all others are anomalous. Only a few land animals are allowed for food, these being limited to the bi-hooved ungulates which are also ruminants. Most animals fall outside this class and are, therefore, inedible. It would not suit Douglas's argument to claim that chewing the cud and having cloven hooves was the sign of the 'normal' animal and that all others were anomalous, for this would not be supported in Genesis 1.

It is true that only certain animals are specifically named (the hyrax, the pig, the camel, the hare), but that is little indication that these were regarded as more of an abomination than others not named. Douglas also seems to have been misled by the significance of the pig in recent Jewish dietary restrictions. Because pork is a staple of diet in many of the societies where Jews live, it is often singled out for discussion. Nevertheless, the Old Testament itself does not emphasize the pig as more polluted than any other animal. It is only one specific example among several.

M.P. Carroll goes beyond Douglas, suggesting that there is a better application of her own theory. One distinction often made in preliterate societies is that between *nature* (desert, jungle) and *culture* (the realm of human beings—cultivated area, dwellings). Meat-eating is a post-Flood phenomenon limited to humans (Gen. 9.3), so that animals which eat meat are trespassing in the realm of 'culture'. Most of the forbidden animals are carnivorous, such as the pig, while all the permitted ones are herbivorous. Even 'leprosy' can be accounted for by this theory, since the 'leprosy' of cloth and buildings is a plant invading the sphere of human beings.

Like Douglas, Carroll makes a number of interesting observations. (Morris also noted that birds of prey may be anomalous because they invade the human sphere [p. 208].) However, even though Carroll avoids some of Douglas's faults, there are problems in his argument. He gives no explanation as to why a wide variety of herbivorous animals are forbidden for food. He also assumes that the ancient Israelites would have classified mould and mildew as plants, which seems to assume an unlikely scientific knowledge on their part.

A.S. Meigs has recently looked again at the question of pollution as a result of her own field work, which led her to make some far-reaching revisions to Douglas's scheme which had become so widely accepted. She finds the idea that things classified as polluting are so regarded because of their ambivalent status especially problematic. For example, she notes that not all bodily emissions are regarded as polluting or, at least, as always polluting. Some which are normally polluting may also have enormous power in certain contexts. The main considerations are whether the substance is perceived as decaying (or as a symbol of decay), whether it is likely to enter one's own body, and whether such access to the body is undesirable. These ideas seem to be present in many taboos on pollution.

Meigs's argument has potential value for some of the Leviticus regulations, especially those relating to genital discharges. On the other hand, her analysis seems to have little bearing on one of the main questions, that of clean and unclean animals. Whether her revisionism is cogent must be debated by social anthropologists, but it illustrates the conviction that pollution rules have social meaning and that the continuing quest to understand them is important.

Despite these criticisms, some of Douglas's points about the meaning of the system in Israelite society remain valid, especially the notion that the system of permitted and forbidden animals was a microcosm of the world according to the Israelite view. The many forbidden animals represented the surrounding nations; the few clean animals, the Israelites; and the sacrificial animals, the priests. Just as Israelites were not to eat certain animals, they were not to mix with other nations. The dietary regulations had both a practical and a symbolic function; symbolically they stood for the fact that Israel was to keep itself free from intercourse with non-Israelites; practically, prohibition of eating certain animals meant that Jews could not socialize with those who ate these animals.

The rules of pollution and purity also drew strict boundaries around the altar and sanctuary. No pollution and no polluted persons were allowed to penetrate into the sacred area. This drawing of clear and rigid boundaries suggests a concern with political as well as social boundaries. Just as the Israelites were concerned about mixing with the surrounding peoples, so their political boundaries may have been threatened by others who claimed the territory for themselves. If so, the message of the rules which, on the surface, might seem arcane ritual turns out to be the expression of a rich symbolic system, significant for understanding the concerns of ancient Israel. This is confirmed in the key passage Lev. 20.22-26 (NJPS translation):

> You shall faithfully observe all My laws and all My regulations, lest the land to which I bring you to settle in spew you out. You shall not follow the practices of the nation that I am driving out before you. For it is because they did all these things that I abhorred them and said to you: You shall possess their land, for I will give it to you to possess...I the Lord am your God who has set you apart from other peoples. So you shall set apart the clean beast from the unclean, the unclean bird from the clean. You shall not draw abomination upon yourselves through beast or bird or anything with which the ground is alive, which I have set apart for you to treat as unclean. You shall be holy to Me, for I the Lord am holy, and I have set you apart from other peoples to be Mine.

Menstruation

This has often been discussed in recent years, especially in works dealing with feminist issues. The regulations about bodily issues in Leviticus 12–15 do not make a particular point about menstruation but deal with it only as one of a number of issues of blood or fluid which are polluting. Nevertheless, most of the other issues are unusual events, whereas the regulations about menstruation would affect all women between puberty and menopause as well as, more indirectly, their families. It is clear that these purity regulations were extremely important to all Israelites of both sexes.

Anthropological studies show that regulations about menstruation often mirror the relationship between the sexes and the place of each sex within the society. Societies in which women have considerable freedom of choice and independence from men will usually reflect this in various customs about ritual purity, including menstruation. Those societies in which women are restricted to a particular place and function and are discouraged from entering the province of men will usually have restrictive regulations about menstruation.

As Mary Douglas has noted, such regulations can have a variety of aims (*Implicit Meanings*, pp. 60-72): (1) to assert male superiority, (2) to assert separate male and female spheres, (3) to attack a rival (especially in polygamous societies), (4) to lay claim to a special relationship (especially in societies where women are more independent). The regulations in Leviticus seem to centre on point (2); some might also argue that point (1) is included, but if so, one would have to ask where the textual support is for asserting that women were considered inferior (although plenty of later texts may be found from which to argue this point). It seems clear that in Israelite society women had a particular sphere and place to which they were restricted. They were not generally allowed to participate in activities which were associated with male Israelites. These customs were not necessarily absolute, since the Old Testament tradition contains stories of exceptional women who broke through the traditional boundaries. But any woman who observed the rules about menstrual pollution would have found her activities severely restricted in certain areas.

A similar purpose seems to be associated with the rules surrounding childbirth (described above). The longer purification time after bearing a daughter would be a symbol indicating that women had an appropriate place in society which was different from that of men.

Summary

Although social anthropology is no substitute for the biblical text, it can be useful, asking new questions, suggesting new lines of enquiry, and formulating and testing new hypotheses. There is always a danger that one may attempt to impose a theory on the biblical material artificially, so that the text is forced to fit the theory. Any theory must be constantly tested against the biblical data. Social anthropology is primarily a heuristic device, useful if handled carefully.

One of the benefits of anthropological study is that it shows that some favoured ideas about the regulations in Leviticus are probably wrong, and that the system made a good deal of sense in the society of ancient Israel. The regulations about purity and pollution may have arisen over many centuries and may have had different functions within the society at different times. From that point of view many of them may be hoary with age, their origins lost in the mists of time. Nevertheless, they form a coherent synchronic system in Leviticus and can embrace many other biblical passages. If there is such an entity as P, it shows a consistent pollution system with an important purpose in the society it envisages. The familiar modern (usually Christian!) polemic which ridicules the pollution system represents only bias and ignorance.

Further Reading

All the main passages in this section are dealt with by Milgrom in *Leviticus 1–16*. He provides discussion and extensive bibliography on most of the points treated. See also the other commentaries. For a recent discussion, see:

P.P. Jenson, *Graded Holiness: A Key to the Priestly Conception of the World* (JSOTSup 106; Sheffield: JSOT Press, 1992).

In addition, see the following, especially for the concept in later Judaism:

J. Neusner, *The Idea of Purity in Ancient Judaism: The Haskell Lectures, 1972–1973*, with a critique and commentary by M. Douglas (SJLA 1;

Leiden: Brill, 1973).

On the anthropological side of pollution and purity, see:

M. Douglas, *Purity and Danger: An Analysis of the Concepts of Pollution and Taboo* (London: Routledge & Kegan Paul, 1966).

J.J. Preston, 'Purification', in *The Encyclopedia of Religion* (London: Macmillan, 1987), XII, pp. 91-100.

However, some elements of Douglas's thinking have been extensively criticized. She rethought her position in some later works, especially in:

M. Douglas, *Implicit Meanings: Essays in Anthropology* (London: Routledge & Kegan Paul, 1975). The two main essays on the question are 'Deciphering a Meal' (pp. 249-75) and 'Self-evidence' (pp. 276-318).

The question of the grid modelling of social relations was taken up in:

M. Douglas, *Natural Symbols: Explorations in Cosmology* (London: Barrie & Jenkins, 1973).

For a critique of Douglas, see the articles she cites in the previous works, as well as especially the following work:

B. Morris, *Anthropological Studies of Religion* (Cambridge: Cambridge University Press, 1987), especially pp. 203-18, 226-34.

A recent treatment of Leviticus 11, attempting to build on Douglas but to avoid her problems, is:

M.P. Carroll, 'One More Time: Leviticus Revisited', *Archives européennes de sociologie* 19 (1978), pp. 339-46.

For the argument that a new basis needs to be laid for understanding pollution, see

A.S. Meigs, 'A Papuan Perspective on Pollution', *Man* 13 (1978), pp. 304-18.

A new study on the clean and unclean animals of Leviticus 11 appeared while my manuscript was in the press and was thus unavailable to me:

W. Houston, *Purity and Monotheism: Clean and Unclean Animals in Biblical Law* (JSOTSup, 140; Sheffield: JSOT Press, 1993).

4

PRIESTS AND LEVITES

THE COMMON NAME for the book of the Bible under consideration is Leviticus, taken from the Greek Septuagint translation via the Latin Vulgate. 'Leviticus' means 'the [book of the] Levites'. No other book is devoted so completely to the priesthood and its activities, yet even though Leviticus is the 'priestly book' *par excellence*, it is not a complete guide either to regulations for the priests or to how the priesthood functioned. Therefore, it cannot be classified as a priestly handbook. Throughout Leviticus, however, especially in chs. 1–10, there is much important information about the priesthood of Israel. As already discussed (see Chapter 1), the schema presented is an idealized one, probably based on a projection of what the priestly authors thought appropriate for a group wandering in the wilderness with a mobile tabernacle. Nevertheless, it is probable that much of the material is traditional and presents some relationship to the actual priesthood under the monarchy.

The Sanctuary

Leviticus does not describe a sanctuary but assumes one. The last chapters of Exodus detail the building of the wilderness tabernacle, and, being conventionally assigned to the P source, they are usually seen as the background for the sanctuary in Leviticus. This is a plausible suggestion, though it requires the acceptance of the theory of a P source. At the very least, it could be said that nothing in Leviticus contradicts a sanctuary like the one described in Exodus: all the references to the sanctuary in Leviticus are consistent with the tabernacle described in Exodus 25–30. This is not surprising since even the general layout of the temple in Ezekiel 40–48 is the same as that in Exodus, despite some important differences.

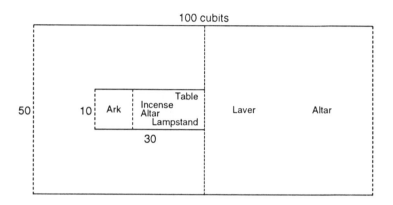

The Concept of the Holy

The existence of the sanctuary assumes the existence of sacred space and sacred time. The idea of 'sacred' or 'holy' is integral to most religious systems. It has been described from a modern point of view in the well-known book by R. Otto, *The Idea of the Holy*; however, this may not help one's understanding of the idea from the ancient Israelites' perspective. The importance of sacred space and time in Israel, and in many other systems, is their function as a 'focusing lens' which concentrates attention on the activities of that time and place and invests them with a particular significance in relationship to the divine (cf. J.Z. Smith). In Israelite literature there is no indication that the sanctuary was holy because of any intrinsic qualities; it was holy only because it had been so designated by God himself. Indeed, if the tabernacle was in theory a portable shrine, the geographical location could not produce the holy space.

The sanctuary and those who served in it were set apart in a special way to be holy. Sacrifices, or at least certain parts of them, also became holy. And those who served at the altar partook of this holiness, being allowed to eat of the holy things which were otherwise forbidden to most Israelites. The priests were as susceptible to impurity and sin as anyone else, and because of their consecration they had to take extra precautions. The high priest in particular was to avoid certain activities (mourning, for example) which might make him impure. The anointing ceremony described in Leviticus 8–9 was to set Aaron and his sons apart to be holy.

Priestly Duties

The main function of the priests was to preside at the altar. In practical terms, priests were butchers. They spent their days slaughtering animals and/or sprinkling blood on the altar, after which they burned parts of the animal or the entire carcass. This seems straightforward and mundane, but it was far from that. These workaday activities were invested with complex symbolism and filled with deep meaning. The actions of cutting, slicing, sprinkling and burning had no intrinsic value, but God had invested them with religious significance. The priests were holy, and what they did was holy work. In fact, their laborious schedule, even if it left them exhausted, overrode the sabbath and holy days. They toiled on the sabbath and were blameless. They delved in blood and guts but were holy. Their ordinary daily activities—butchering, baking, working, eating, all activities parallel to those of other Israelites—were pronounced sacred.

Priests, must, logically, have had other functions as well as those at the altar, as Leviticus itself indicates. For example, the priest had to pronounce on whether a person or object infected with 'leprosy' was clean or not (Leviticus 13–14). One might extrapolate from this that one of the priestly responsibilities was to rule on cultic and purity matters, as Hag. 2.11-13 seems to indicate. Elsewhere, the Old Testament suggests that there were still other responsibilities. According to Deuteronomy (where they are called the 'Levitical priests') they were to act as judges (Deut. 17.8-12; 19.17; 21.5). They were responsible for promulgating the law of Moses (Deut. 31.9-13) and, in general, to be teachers (Deut. 24.8; 27.9-10). In other words, they were responsible for religious law, and even for much of what might be categorized as civil law, according to Deuteronomy. Leviticus is silent on much of this. It may have presupposed such activity, but it is not certain. It is plausible that the priests were supposed to do much more than just serve at the altar, and the analogies of other religious systems and priests supports this; but Leviticus—for whatever reason—saw no need to expound on this question explicitly.

Priestly Dues

Sacrificial Portions
As already discussed (see Chapter 2), one of the special concerns of Leviticus 6–7 is that of the sacrificial portions which went to the priests. Some offerings (the burnt offering in particular) were burned entirely, but for most only certain parts of the animal went on the altar while the rest was divided between the offerer and the offering priest or went entirely to the priest. Two portions of most offerings from the herd or flock belonged to the priests. The breast was presented as the *těnûfāh* before Yahweh and then given to all the priesthood ('Aaron and his sons'); the right thigh was presented as the *těrûmāh* and allocated to the offering priest (Lev. 7.29-36). What do these terms mean? Their precise meaning is much disputed.

It has been customary in English translations to translate *těnûfāh* as 'wave offering' and *těrûmāh* as 'heave offering'. This was how they were interpreted in rabbinic literature (*m. Men.* 5.6). A correct understanding of the offerings may have been preserved among the rabbis, but this is not necessarily the case. The earliest rabbinic discussion is found in the Mishnah, a book which was compiled long after the temple had ceased to exist. Other rabbinic references are even later. The early translations into Greek do not give a consistent rendering which would help towards the understanding of these offerings. It is hardly surprising, therefore, that some modern attempts to understand the terms differ from the traditional ones.

The term *těnûfāh* was applied especially to the thigh of the sacrifices of well-being which went to the priest, but it was also used in other passages. In trying to understand this offering, Milgrom points to two common denominators of the various objects labelled *těnûfāh*: (1) any offering still in the possession of its owner before sacrifice (especially the sacrifice of well-being) requires dedication; (2) most sacrificial gifts whose composition or mode of offering is outside the norm require additional sanctification.

Clues have been sought in the supposed etymology of the word, but there is no agreement on its origin. Akkadian *nūpta* means 'additional payment'; if it is cognate, it might suggest that *těnûfāh* has nothing to do with a type of motion. Fitting with the meaning of the Akkadian word is the proposed Arabic cognate *nawf*, 'surplus'. Milgrom notes that the *těnûfāh* offerings were piled on the hands of Aaron and his sons (Exod. 29.24). Using this description, philology, and the analogy of certain offerings in Egypt, he suggests that the word refers to the ritual of raising or lifting the object to dedicate it as an offering to God. In any case, the motion was not 'waving'. Anderson objected to this interpretation, however, noting that the cognate evidence of *nāfāh* which Milgrom cites from Aramaic and Syriac better fits the concept of 'wave' than Milgrom's 'elevate'. Anderson rejects any reference to motion at all, but thinks that the *těnûfāh* is something done in addition which would fit well into Israel's sacrificial cult.

With regard to *těrûmāh*, all occurrences of the word suggest that it was a gift intended for God or the priest. In contrast to the *těnûfāh* offering, there is no ceremony in the temple; whatever act is performed is done outside the sanctuary. The translation 'heave' offering, derived from *rwm* 'raise, be high' is questionable. However, the Hebrew verb in the *hiphil* formation means 'dedicate' or 'set aside'. This has been seen as connected with Akkadian *rāmu* 'give a gift', but the origin and history of the Akkadian word is complex (see Anderson). This makes the use of it problematic. As with *těnûfāh* there is no reason to assume particular

movements of the hands. Whatever the precise significance of
the name, *tĕrûmāh* applies primarily to the breast of the
sacrificial animals which was given to the priest.

One problem is that some passages seem to assume that the
presiding priest received the sacrificial portions (Lev. 7.32-33;
cf. Lev. 7.7, 9-10), whereas others seem to presuppose that
they went to the priesthood as a whole to be divided up (Lev.
7.30-31). This discrepancy may be explained by cultic
developments: the portions may originally have gone to the
presiding priest when the shrine was a small affair, but a
subsequent increase in the priesthood and in the volume of
worshippers would have required changes.

Vows
Leviticus 27 has an important discussion about support for the
priesthood. Much of this chapter is devoted to the question of
vows and consecration of objects and property to God (Lev.
27.1-29). It was possible to dedicate human beings, animals,
houses, and land to God. If the dedicated object was a human,
the person had to be redeemed by money. The valuation of the
redemption money was according to age and sex. If an animal
suitable for offering had been vowed, it had to be sacrificed: no
substitution was allowed. (Any attempt at substitution meant
that both the original vow and the substitute became dedicated
to God.) However, if it were an unclean animal, it had to be
redeemed by its valuation plus twenty per cent. A house could
be redeemed by paying its value plus twenty per cent.

Land was valued in relation to the jubilee year, taking the
number of harvests remaining until the jubilee into account
and setting value according to that number. Inherited land
could then be redeemed for its valuation plus twenty per cent.
If the owner did not redeem the land and it was sold, however,
it was not longer in his power to redeem. Instead it became
priestly property. According to Deut. 18.1-2, Levites (including
priests) were not to own land as individuals. Apparently,
though, the temple and priesthood could own land jointly. (We
know that priestly ownership of land was practised in the
Second Temple period.)

Land which had been purchased (as distinct from inherited)

did not, however, belong perpetually to the purchaser but reverted to the original owner in the jubilee. Thus, if such land was consecrated, it would still go back to the owner in the jubilee, so its valuation without any addition was given to the priests.

Devoted things (*ḥērem*) belonged solely to God and were not to be made use of by man (Lev. 27.28-29). They could not be sold or redeemed. Even a devoted human being was to be put to death. This last statement is puzzling because normally the human beings who belonged to God were to be redeemed. For example, the firstborn were to be redeemed for money because their place was taken by the Levites (Num. 3.5-13; 18.15). It seems unlikely than an Israelite would be allowed to devote another Israelite or even a slave to God in this way. Therefore, it is unclear who the 'devoted person' might be who would be put to death; however, there are several examples of prisoners of war being slain at God's command, and this might be what was meant (cf. Josh. 6.17-25; 10.24-27; 1 Samuel 15).

Firstlings and Firstfruits
Leviticus mentions the firstborn only briefly (in 27.26-27). Other passages of priestly instruction expand on this (Exod. 13.11-15; 34.19-20; Num. 18.15-18): all clean animals were to be offered at the altar, with the appropriate portions burned, but the rest of the meat going to the priests. The treatment of unclean animals was more complicated: there seem to have been more than one set of instructions. It is clear that they were normally to be redeemed, though Exod. 34.20 says that this was to be with a lamb, whereas Lev. 27.27 states that redemption is to be according to their monetary value plus twenty per cent. Similarly, if they are not redeemed, Lev. 27.27 prescribes that they should be sold for their assessed value, with the money going to the temple personnel. Exod. 34.20, on the other hand, says the animal's neck should be broken.

Firstfruits are mentioned in Leviticus (2.14-16) and elsewhere (especially Num. 18.12-14; Deut. 18.4; 26.1-11). The amount is not precisely stated, but the impression given is that donations of these were to be made to the priesthood as well as the other priestly gifts.

Tithes

Tithing serves as a useful example to illustrate the difficulties of understanding both the Old Testament laws and their application in Israelite society. Few other subjects have more information in the OT literature or in early Jewish literature.

Little is said about tithes in Leviticus—only a few brief verses at Lev. 27.30-33. Yet the main support of the priesthood would logically come from the tithes. Priestly portions of sacrifices or vows would not have been sufficient to sustain an active priesthood under normal circumstances. Two sources of tithes are indicated: (1) the produce of the field—grain, fruits, and the like; (2) the livestock. The vegetable produce is only mentioned in passing here, though it might be expected to be the same as indicated in Num. 18.25-32.

The tithe of animals is not referred to anywhere else in the Pentateuch. They were to be tithed apparently by running them past and cutting out every tenth animal, regardless of whether it was good or bad. If the owner tried to substitute an animal, not only was the original tithe animal still considered as belonging to Yahweh but also the substitute, which discouraged substitution. Nothing is said about how the tithe was to be used. From other passages (2 Chron. 31.6, for example) it may be presumed to go to the priests as a part of their income.

A number of questions arise. Why is not the tithe of animals referred to elsewhere in the Old Testament except in 2 Chron. 31.6? How was the tithing to be carried out? If the entire herd or flock was run by each year, the breeding stock would become, literally, decimated. Would it just have been the new crop of calves, kids, and lambs each time? This would make sense, but no instruction is given. Why? It may be that this was only a theoretical law which was never put into practice. To give the firstborn of each breeding animal would equal roughly ten per cent, so how was the tithe related to the command about the firstborn?

The whole question of tithing in ancient Israel is surrounded by difficulties of understanding and of relating the literary

tradition to the actual situation. Num. 18.21-32 states that all
the tithes were to go to the Levites. The Levites in turn were to
tithe this tithe and give it to the priests. Neh. 10.38-39 (Eng.
10.37-38) seems to give a similar picture. Deut. 12.17-19 and
14.22-29, on the other hand, speaks of eating the tithe in the
'place that the Lord your God will choose'. If the distance was
too great, the tithe could be converted to money and brought to
the sanctuary to be exchanged for food for a feast. All
members of the household were to take part in the feast, and
the Levite was to be included (Deut. 12.18). In the third year,
however, the tithe was to be brought into the settlements and
given to the Levites, the stranger, the fatherless and the
widow.

How do these instructions relate to one another? It is not
clear that they do; some of the differences may have belonged
to an idealized cult which some groups wanted to impose but
which was in fact never practised. There is, however, some
information on what was done during the Second Temple
period. The tradition seemed to envisage two tithes: a first tithe
to the priests and a second tithe which was used to travel to
Jerusalem at the annual festivals (Tob. 1.6-8 [Codex
Sinaiticus]; *Jub.* 32.8-15; Mishnah, tractates *Ma'aserot* and
Ma'aser Sheni). There was also a poor man's tithe (Deut.
14.28-29), which seems to have been regarded as making
different use of the second tithe in the third and sixth years of
a seven-year cycle (cf. also *m. Pe'ah* 8.2). However, some
sources indicate that three full tithes were paid in the third
and sixth years (Tob. 1.6-8 [Codex Vaticanus]; Josephus, *Ant.*
4.8.22 §240). The one comment on the tithe of cattle indicates
that it was used as second tithe (*m. Bek.* 9.1-8). From what
little indications exist, the tithes were paid directly to the
priests, rather than to the Levites who then tithed to the
priests (Tob. 1.6-8; Jdt. 11.13; Josephus, *Ant.* 20.9.2 §206).

In sum, despite much data from the Old Testament and
later Jewish sources, information on tithing is still very confusing. That there was a tithe of vegetable produce for the
priests is likely since such a practice was widespread in the
ancient Near East. It does not seem likely that the cereal
offerings and various portions of sacrificial animals would be

sufficient support for a priesthood, especially one presiding at a
national shrine with many visitors and pilgrims each year.
Beyond this firm inference the matter becomes more
speculative.

Levites

Leviticus mentions the Levites only once (Lev. 25.32-34) but
their existence is taken for granted. Scholars have generally
assumed that this passage should be fitted in with such passages as Num. 8.5-26, 18.6-7, and perhaps even Ezekiel 44–45.
The situation does seem consistent in the 'priestly' stratum of
the Pentateuch: only the sons of Aaron were to preside at the
altar; only they were priestly in the true sense of the term. The
Levites were an inferior clergy whose responsibility was the
care of the physical tabernacle and serving the priests and the
cultic service. This contrasts with the view in Deuteronomy
which seems to assume that all Levites (called 'Levitical
priests') were priests and should be allowed to serve at the
altar. The historical reality is generally thought to be related to
that period immediately following Josiah's reform. When the
Levites serving at country shrines were brought to Jerusalem,
there were too many to serve at the altar, while the traditional
Jerusalem priesthood was not of a mind to share this privilege
anyway. Thus, the Levites became a sort of second-class
clergy, occupied with the tasks of physical serving but
excluded from service at the altar.

Anointing and Consecration of the Priests

Leviticus 8–9 describes a ceremony in which Aaron and his
sons were anointed and consecrated to their offices. There is
agreement that this was a priestly fiction; that is, these
chapters do not describe an actual event involving Aaron and
Moses in the wilderness of Sinai. On the other hand, these
chapters may relate something about priestly belief or practice. Leviticus seems to envisage the anointing of Aaron and
his sons as a one-time event, setting apart their descendants to
the priesthood for ever, as does Exodus (29.9; 40.15). However,

every new high priest was customarily designated by anointing (Lev. 6.15 [Eng. 6.22]).

The lengthy ritual described in Leviticus 8–9 has many characteristics of what is known as a 'rite of passage' (van Gennep). This is an anthropological term for rites which take place as a person passes from one stage of life to another, such as from boyhood to manhood or girlhood to womanhood. There is first a rite of separation, next a transitional rite during which the person is in a 'liminal' state ('on the threshold' between one phase and another). There may be dangers while one is in this liminal state, and rituals have to be performed carefully to protect the person undergoing the transition. In the case of Aaron and his sons, they were undergoing the passage from 'common' to 'sacred'. Various purification and burnt offerings and washings were performed, a special ordination offering was carried out (8.22-29), and the anointing performed. Those involved were then required to remain a week segregated in the tent of meeting (transitional rite). The final act was a ritual of incorporation, in this case consisting of sacrifices and ceremonies on the eighth day (Leviticus 9). Thus, the ceremony of consecration in Leviticus 8–9 parallels rites of passage known both from preliterate modern societies and from examples in modern Western culture.

The Deaths of Nadab and Abihu

The chapters on the anointing are immediately followed by ch. 10, which describes the deaths of Aaron's sons Nadab and Abihu for offering 'alien fire' (*'ēš zārāh*) on the altar. The episode is puzzling since the 'sin' of the two sons is never clearly indicated, with the result that the passage has generated many explanations in later Judaism (Hecht; Kirschner). Thus, as with the golden calf episode, one must ask what lies behind the story. Those who date this part of Leviticus late usually look for some event in the exilic or post-exilic period. For example, Noth thought he saw in the background some internal disputes between different priestly groups. However, others ascribe the background to one or other event during the time of the monarchy. Milgrom suggests that the chapter is a polemic against private offerings of incense. There are textual and archaeological indications that it was common for Israelites to offer incense to God in their homes and elsewhere outside the Jerusalem temple. Those who believed in cult centralization would have disapproved of this practice. A graphic story like that in Leviticus 10 would serve as a salutary reminder that private incense offerings were fraught with danger.

Priestly Theology

It has been common for scholars to disparage the place of the priesthood (whether explicitly or implicitly), especially in contrast to the prophets. The priests were concerned with mechanical ritual, empty ceremony. By contrast, the heart of religion was the living word of God and its ethical meaning, as known from the recitation of God's acts and propounded by the prophets, and so on. This is an oversimplification, but it illustrates a common problem. Even so eminent a scholar as von Rad found little to praise in the priestly writers.

Nothing approaching a complete description of the cult of ancient Israel exists. There are some descriptions of cultic ceremonies on some occasions, but it is not known how the cult was carried on from day to day. Did prayers accompany some or all the sacrifices? Was there singing? Many of the psalms are thought to have originated in the cult, either as prayers or as songs, but this may only be inferred. Later Jewish texts suggest that the temple and its ritual had great symbolic meaning for the participants. But this may only be guessed at, since the later texts may not give any indication about earlier views.

What must be acknowledged is that the purpose of ritual texts was to give a careful description of ritual. Leviticus may not be a ritual text as such, but it has many characteristics in common with them. Ritual texts, however, do not explain the theological or religious significance of the ritual. This may be found in other kinds of text, or may be preserved as oral tradition. The ritual itself may convey much of the meaning for those who participate in it. Although the main duty of the priest, as noted above, was to serve at the altar, priests would have been one of the few groups of Israelites with leisure to devote their minds to intellectual tasks. It would hardly be surprising if many of the psalms and even the wisdom writings arose from within the priesthood. That the priests had an interest beyond the cult proper is indicated by the variety of material found throughout Leviticus about society and the conduct of life in its broadest sense.

In short, it would be a mistake to assume that the priests were only repetitively and mechanically going through empty rituals. On the contrary, there is reason to believe that the rites had considerable spiritual meaning for the priests and for the ordinary Israelites. One may only guess at this meaning, but it is certain that it was there. The priests were probably the first theologians in ancient Israel.

Further Reading

General studies of the priests and Levites can be found in:

A. Cody, *A History of Old Testament Priesthood* (AnBib 35; Rome: Pontifical Biblical Institute, 1969).

A.H.J. Gunneweg, *Leviten und Priester: Hauptlinien der Traditionsbildung und Geschichte des israelitisch-jüdischen Kultpersonals* (FRLANT 89; Göttingen: Vandenhoeck & Ruprecht, 1965).

P.P. Jenson, *Graded Holiness: A Key to the Priestly Conception of the World* (JSOTup 106; Sheffield: JSOT Press, 1992) chs. 2, 3, and 5.

See also articles on 'Levites' and 'priests' in *Theological Dictionary of the Old Testament* (*Theologische Wörterbuch zum Alten Testament*).

On the concept of the sacred, see:

R. Otto, *The Idea of the Holy* (Oxford: Oxford University Press, 1923).

J.Z. Smith, 'The Bare Facts of Ritual', *History of Religions* 20 (1980), pp. 112-27; reprinted in *Imagining Religion: From Babylon to Jonestown* (Chicago Studies in the History of Judaism; Chicago: University of Chicago Press, 1982), pp. 53-65.

—*To Take Place: Toward Theory in Ritual* (Chicago Studies in the History of Judaism; Chicago: University of Chicago Press, 1987).

See also articles on 'sacred and profane', 'sacred space', and 'sacred time', in the *Encyclopaedia of Religion*.

The major study of tithing in the Old Testament is still:

O. Eissfeldt, *Erstlinge und Zehnten im Alten Testament: Ein Beitrag zur Geschichte des israelitisch-jüdischen Kultus* (Beiträge zur Wissenschaft vom Alten Testament 22; Leipzig: J.C. Hinrichs, 1917).

On rites of passage, see:

A. van Gennep, *The Rites of Passage* (London: Routledge & Kegan Paul, 1960).

On the later interpretation of the Nadab and Abihu incident, see:

R. Hecht, 'Patterns of Exegesis in Philo's Interpretation of Leviticus', *Studia Philonica* 6 (1979–80), pp. 77-155.

R. Kirschner, 'Rabbinic and Philonic Exegesis of the Nadab and Abihu Incident (Lev. 10:1-6)', *JQR* 73 (1982–83), pp. 375-93.

On the question of theology, see:

Milgrom, *Leviticus 1–16*, pp. 42-51.

G. von Rad, *Theology of the Old Testament*. I. *The Theology of Israel's Historical Traditions* (Edinburgh: Oliver & Boyd, 1962), pp. 232-79.

5

'YOU SHALL BE HOLY AS I AM HOLY'
THE HOLINESS CODE

LEVITICUS 17–26 IS USUALLY distinguished from the rest of the book and designated the holiness code (see Chapter 1); Leviticus 27 is viewed as a later appendix. These chapters give a different perspective from Leviticus 1–16: the subject matter is sometimes similar, but the point of view is more that of the layman than the priest. A number of sections are devoted to clear themes: the shedding and treatment of blood (17), prohibited sexual relations (18), regulations for the priests (21–22), festivals (23), sabbatical and jubilee years (25), and blessings and cursings (26). Other chapters, especially 19 and 20, have a miscellaneous character in terms of modern ideas about proper organization. Yet even those chapters which seem to be devoted to a single subject do not always show a consistent internal structure and may have originated from a coalescence of individual traditions.

Leviticus 17.1-16:
The Shedding of Blood and its Treatment

It was envisaged that all slaughter was to be done at the altar so that the blood could be dashed against the altar and the fat burned on it (17.3-7). Thus, all slaughter of animals for food would take place in a sacrificial context, and no butchering or consumption of meat could be done away from the shrine. How could this stipulation be carried out in practical terms? This difficulty is highlighted by Deut. 12.20-25, which seemed to change just such a regulation when it stated that profane slaughter was allowed, as long as the blood was drained out of the animal. This means that Leviticus 17 must either be an idealized system divorced from reality or have envisaged a society small enough in numbers and territory to allow a trip to the altar and back within a day or so.

The corollary to this is that all sacrifice was to be done at the central shrine. Although no specific site is mentioned in Leviticus, it is clear that only one altar was envisaged, the context being the (fictional) tabernacle in the wilderness. Sacrifices were not to be carried out elsewhere (17.7-9). The exception to this rule about slaughter at the altar was the case of clean wild animals or birds which could be hunted, killed and eaten apart from the shrine as long as the blood was drained out onto the earth (17.13-14).

Blood itself is a central element in this chapter. The life of both human beings and animals is in their blood. For that reason, blood should not be eaten but dashed on the altar or poured on the ground and covered with dust. Blood functions as a potent symbol within the sacrificial cult and has to be given due weight in any theological discussion of the meaning of the cult. For the same reason that blood was not to be eaten, that which dies of itself or is killed by animals was not to be eaten: it polluted the eater (17.15-16). Whether such eating was strictly forbidden or only frowned upon is debatable.

Leviticus 18.1-30: Forbidden Sexual Relations

Much of this chapter covers what is usually referred to as incest, that is, sexual relations forbidden because of the closeness of kinship of the persons involved. However, other sexual acts are also mentioned. The following are forbidden to the Israelite male.

First, sexual acts 'with his own flesh' (near of kin): mother or step-mother (Lev. 18.6-8); sister, half-sister, step-sister, or sister-in-law (Lev. 18.9, 11, 16); daughter-in-law (Lev. 18.10, 15); aunt (Lev. 18.12-14); a woman and her daughter or granddaughter (Lev. 18.17). Other regulations seem more concerned with what was deemed appropriate: not to take a wife's sister as rival wife (Lev. 18.18); not to indulge in sexual intercourse during the menstrual period (Lev. 18.19) or with the neighbour's wife (Lev. 18.20), with another male (Lev. 18.22) or with animals (Lev. 18.23). It was forbidden to offer one's children to Molech (Lev. 18.21).

The prohibited relations were justified by an appeal to the 'abominations' of the Egyptians and Canaanites (Lev. 18.1-5, 24-30). There is no evidence that these peoples were less moral than the Israelites, or that their sexual practices were necessarily very different. (The notorious brother–sister marriages of ancient Egypt see to have been limited to the royal family.) There may have been differences in definition of what constituted incest among these peoples compared with Israel, as might be expected, but they had their own strict social codes. The 'abominations of the Egyptians and Canaanites' are a fiction which still persists, especially with regard to Canaanite religion.

Sexual relations are at the heart of social practice within any community. Each society has strict views about which kinds are allowed and which are not; these views may change over time and—human nature and passions being what they are—rules are often breached, but they still exist even in the most seemingly promiscuous of societies. Indeed, promiscuity in one area of a society may be matched by great rigidity in another area.

Social anthropologists have found that laws about permitted and forbidden sexual relationships are an important clue to attitudes towards relatives and outsiders. In many preliterate societies elaborate codes govern marriage. Often these prescribe exogamy, even if the only source of wives or husbands may be an enemy tribe. Israel's rules here are lenient (despite the claim that 'the Canaanites' allowed sexual relations with close of kin), allowing even first cousins to marry. Israel was thus an endogamous society. This fits with their emphasis on rigid barriers to non-Israelites. Easy marriage between groups internally would, of course, help to prevent the need for marriage to outsiders.

Leviticus 19.1–20.27: Miscellaneous Laws

The term 'miscellaneous' is used to indicate a modern
perspective; no doubt the ancient authors/compilers had their
own views and may have arranged the material according to
a logical pattern from their standpoint. This section has a
number of parallels with the covenant code (Exod. 21.1–
23.33) and Deut. 12.26, as well as with the laws known
elsewhere in the ancient Near East. The themes of Lev. 20.10-
21 are also parallel to those of Leviticus 16, although there
seems to have been no direct borrowing either way. It has been
suggested by a number of commentators (e.g. Patrick) that
the regulations of 19.1–20.9 have parallels with the decalogue.
It is true that the contents of some of the ten commandments
are echoed here (Lev. 19.11-12/Exod. 20.7, 13 for example),
but this seems to be fortuitous. There is no obvious relationship
between the structure and wording of Leviticus 19–20 and
the decalogue. Comparison of the Old Testament and the legal
material elsewhere in the ancient Near East suggests that
much traditional exhortative material was widespread in the
area. Each people selected, modified, refined, and developed
the tradition in its own way, but a significant overlap is still
easy to observe in the extant literature (see Chapter 1).

Leviticus 21.1-24: Laws on the Priesthood

The presumption was that all Israel was to be holy; but the
priests had to be even more rigorous. They were not allowed to
defile themselves by contact with a corpse through participating in funerals other than of close blood relatives: mother,
father, son, daughter, brother, or an unmarried sister (Lev.
21.1-4). They were not to carry out mourning rites by dis-
figuring their hair, beards, or flesh (Lev. 21.5-6). They were
not allowed to marry a harlot or divorcee, and the priest's
daughter who became a harlot was to be burned (Lev. 21.7-9).
    The Old Testament as a whole does not say much about a
high priest, though we know that the high priest became very
important in Second Temple times. Leviticus does envisage a
high priest, however, as this chapter shows (Lev. 21.10-15).

This person had been anointed by the sacred oil (see Chapter 4 for further comments on this). He was not to participate in a funeral, even for a close relative, or engage in mourning rites of any kind. He was to marry only a virgin of his own people.

The regulations about those who could preside at the altar were also rigorous (Lev. 21.16-23). Just as animals to be sacrificed were to be without physical defect, so the officiating priests were to be without physical blemish. A number of these defects are mentioned, though they may be only representative. Nevertheless, even priests whose physical deformity or disease prevented the carrying out of their priestly duties were allowed to eat of the priestly gifts.

Leviticus 22.1-33: Regulations about the Sacred Gifts

Certain portions of the sacrificial animals and other offerings were to go to the priests (see Chapter 4). These were sacred and to be eaten only by those qualified and only under certain conditions. The priests and their families who were in a state of purity, and they alone, were to partake of them (Lev. 22.3-16). The various sorts of uncleanness are specified, but these do not differ from those already mentioned (see Chapter 3). Laypersons were not to eat of these holy things. Hired servants also were forbidden to do so, but slaves owned by the priests were considered a part of the family and could eat them. The priestly portions were prohibited to the daughter of a priest who married a layman, unless she became divorced or a widow and returned to her father's house. If a layman unwittingly ate of the sacred gifts, he was to restore them, together with an additional twenty per cent of their value (Lev. 22.14).

All offerings were to be of whole, normal animals without major physical defects (Lev. 22.17-25). Anything which was blind, injured, maimed, or had certain sorts of disease was rejected. Neither was a castrated animal to be accepted (the implication being that Israelites did not castrate their animals, contrary to the normal practice of others around them). An animal with a limb extraordinarily short or long could be accepted for a free-will offering but not for a vow. This was the

only explicit concession made about blemishes, though how
these regulations might have been interpreted in practice is
unknown.

A newborn animal was not to be sacrificed until it had been
with its mother seven days (Lev. 22.26), nor was it and its
mother to be sacrificed on the same day (22.27). Any thanksgiving offering had to be eaten on the day it was offered; anything left over was to be burnt (22.29-30, in agreement with
7.15).

Leviticus 23.1-44: The Festivals

Matters regrading the festivals are dealt with in Chapter 6
below.

Leviticus 24.1-9: Lampstand and Bread of Presence

The first part of this chapter relates to the area inside the holy
place but in front of the curtain separating the Holy of Holies
(see diagram in Chapter 4). A very pure olive oil was to be
provided to keep the lampstand burning continually (Lev.
24.2-4). There was also to be a table on which twelve loaves
(together with frankincense) were to be placed each sabbath.
The frankincense was evidently burned at the end of the
week, and the priests were allowed to eat the loaves. This was
known as the bread of presence or show bread.

Leviticus 24.10-23: Blasphemy

At times within Leviticus there occurs a narrative rather
than a specific law. In such cases, the episode in question
seems to have been intended to explain what should be done by
example rather than by direct instruction. In this passage, an
Israelite whose father was Egyptian used God's name in a
blasphemous way. He was put in custody until God could be
consulted. God's reply was that the man should be stoned by
the entire community. In the future, anyone blaspheming
with God's name was likewise to be executed by stoning.
Within this section there is an inset paragraph about life and

reciprocation of punishment, otherwise known as the *lex talionis*.

The Lex Talionis

Leviticus 24.17-22 stresses the importance of life, especially human life. One who kills another person is to be executed. The person who kills an animal must make restitution. The principle is also stated that injuries were to be compensated by a reciprocal injury to the perpetrator—the famous 'eye for an eye and a tooth for a tooth'. This law has often been misunderstood as a primitive barbaric practice, which embarrassed legislators later did their best to soften.

In fact, the earlier principle was that a person injuring another was to pay compensation. In the case of an extended family or community, that was the simplest way of handling the matter. The injured party, or the family, received some benefit. The *lex talionis* was an important advance in jurisprudence for two reasons: first, it made everyone equal before the law. The rich could not get away with the crime of injuring another simply by making monetary payment. The 'eye for an eye' principle was a great leveller. Secondly, the law marked the stage at which the tribe or state took over the function of justice from the local community.

Leviticus 25.1-55: The Sabbatical and Jubilee Years

Matters regarding the sabbatical and jubilee years are dealt with in Chapter 6 below.

Leviticus 26.1-46: Concluding Blessings and Cursings

An appropriate literary closure of a book such as Leviticus is a section demonstrating the consequences of heeding or ignoring the commands contained in it. A similar conclusion may be found in Deuteronomy 28. Here in Leviticus 26 the blessings for obedience come first (26.3-13), with promises of peace, plenty, and fertility. The section given over to the curses for disobedience is longer and more clearly structured (26.14-38). Five sections are marked off with the phrase, 'If you [still] disobey, I will punish you sevenfold' or similar words (26.14-

17, 18-20, 21-22, 23-26, 27-38). The aim seems to have been to create a crescendo effect, so that the longer the Israelites refused to obey, the stronger became the punishments, multiplying sevenfold each time. This does not seem to have been carried through consistently, although there is a climax in the exile from the land. Finally, hope is expressed for repentance and a return from captivity (Lev. 26.39-45).

Such blessings and curses are well known from other ancient Near Eastern literature. International treaties usually ended with a list of blessings and, especially, curses for disobedience. The so-called 'law codes' often included a similar section. For example, the epilogue to the Code of Hammurabi spelled out how the gods would punish the king in various ways for not heeding the marvellous laws which had just been listed. As with the list in Leviticus 26, the curses tended to dominate, with the blessings listed only briefly. Leviticus 26.31-45 ends with reference to an exile and return, which led many scholars to claim that this showed knowledge of the exile of the Jews in 587/586 BCE and their return in 538 BCE. This may be a correct interpretation, but it should be noted that one of the traditional punishments in comparable texts was that the people of the land would be taken captive (Code of Hammurabi xxvi.73-80; xxviii.19-23 for example).

Leviticus 27.1-34: An Appendix on Vows and Tithes

Generally, it is felt that Leviticus 27 does not fit the structure of H which should, logically, end with ch. 6. It seems to be a later addition, added as an appendix to H. For a discussion of its contents, see Chapter 4.

Further Reading

For bibliography on law in Israel and in the ancient Near East, see Chapter 1.

On the blessings and curses of ancient Near Eastern treaties, see:
D.J. McCarthy, *Treaty and Covenant: A Study in Form in the Ancient Oriental Documents and in the Old Testament* (AnBib 21A; Rome: Pontifical Biblical Institute, 2nd edn, 1978), pp. 172-87.
On the Canaanites, see:
N.P. Lemche, *The Canaanites and their Land: The Tradition of the Canaanites* (JSOTSup 110; Sheffield: JSOT Press, 1991).

6

SACRED TIME:
THE CULTIC CALENDAR

THE CONCEPT OF SACRED TIME is found in most, if not all, religions and is taken for granted in most forms of liturgical worship. It was not simply how God was worshipped but also when. God had marked off certain periods of time as different—as holy—with rules as to how they should and should not be used. Several sections of Leviticus are concerned with the proper times for various observances: the weekly sabbath and the annual festivals, as well as the sabbatical year and the jubilee year.

The Calendar

The determination of times—the calendar—is important to regulations about festivals and holy times but, surprisingly, the calendar is nowhere discussed in the Old Testament. It seems to have been taken for granted, and was mentioned only in passing.

In some texts, the months are listed only by number: 'seventh month', 'first month', and so on. Occasionally, the old Hebrew month names are mentioned, although only some of these are known. Mainly, when the actual name of a month is used in the Old Testament, the later Jewish name which had been borrowed from the Babylonians is used.

Babylonian Name	*Old Hebrew Name*
Nisan	Abib
Iyyar (not mentioned in OT)	Ziv
Sivan	
Tammuz (not mentioned in OT)	
Av (not mentioned in OT)	
Elul	
Tishri (not mentioned in OT)	Ethanim
Marchesvan (not mentioned in OT)	Bul
Kislev	
Tebeth	
Shebat	
Adar	

The New Moon

The day of the new moon, that is, the first day of the month, was important, primarily because it signalled to people at large the reckoning of the new month. In fact, the word for new moon (*ḥōdeš*) is also the usual Hebrew word for 'month'. Although the new moon in its calendrical function is mentioned in Leviticus, it is not labelled a holy day. Indeed, there is no passage in the Old Testament which explicitly makes it a holy day, nor was it treated as such in anything known from later Judaism. Some scholars have thought that it was one of the original holy days, perhaps even a forerunner of the sabbath; if so, this function has either been edited out of the Old Testament tradition or that aspect of the new moon day had ceased when the Old Testament tradition was being formed. Thus, the new moon is not discussed anywhere in Leviticus.

Beginning of the New Year

It is often asserted that in pre-exilic times the beginning of the year was in the autumn—in what later became the seventh month or Tishri. This coincides with the traditional new year or Rosh ha-Shanah of Jews today. An autumnal new year has been taken for granted and major theories built on this assumption. In fact, the supposed P source states that the year began in the spring (Exod. 12.2), with the month of Nisan. D.J.A. Clines has argued cogently that the spring new year was the common way of reckoning the calendar in pre-exilic times.

The Sabbath

The word 'sabbath' is derived from the Hebrew root *šbt* which means 'rest, cessation'. The basic characteristic of the sabbath was that no work (*mĕlā'kāh*) of any kind was to be done. What made up that prohibited work is not precisely stated anywhere. Outside Leviticus, one passage notes that work is also prohibited on the holy days except 'that which each person must eat' (Exod. 12.16), suggesting that the preparation of food was allowed on these annual sabbaths but not on the weekly sabbath.

Much later, certain other types of activity were allowable by some groups of Jews but forbidden by others. For example, one could aid the 'ox in the ditch' on the sabbath according to general custom (Mt. 12.11), though other Jews actually forbade it (Damascus Document [CD] 11.13-14). The saving of human life seems to have been almost universally allowable (cf. CD 11.16-17), but even here there was a qualification: in one instance, a group of Jews refused to fight in self-defence on the sabbath (1 Macc. 2.32-38), a fact which caused others to make the explicit decision that defensive warfare was permissible on the sabbath, but not offensive (1 Macc. 2.39-41). This custom was taken advantage of by some Gentile generals, who used the sabbath to extend and strengthen their siege works, knowing that they could proceed unmolested as long as they did not attack the Jewish defenders directly (Josephus, *War* 1.7.3 §146).

How much later practice can be projected back to the time and mind of the writers of Leviticus is arguable. No doubt there were views among the priestly writers about what was permitted and what was not, but whether this reflected observance among Jews as a whole is not clear.

The sabbath seems to have had a long history in Israel and was not invented by the priestly writers; but it is difficult to say how far back the development of sabbath observance may be traced. It was once common to regard the sabbath as primarily a post-exilic innovation. Sabbath observance is emphasized mainly in exilic and post-exilic texts (Isaiah 56; Neh. 13.15-22 for example). There is also the question of the sabbath passage here in Leviticus 23, since from a form-critical point of view, v. 3 appears to be a later insertion and not part of the original list. Yet some texts, generally acknowledged to be pre-exilic, presuppose sabbath observance (Hos. 2.13 [Eng. 2.11]; Amos 8.5; Isa. 1.13), indicating that it was known and observed in some circles as early as the eighth century BC. Arguments have been made for an earlier observance, based on such passages as Exod. 23.12, 34.21 (cf. 2 Kgs 4.23). Although it does not seem to be attested as early as some of the annual festivals, some scholars argue that it goes far back in Israel's history and is not a late development (see Andreasen).

The question of the origin of the sabbath is a difficult one (Andreasen, Shafer). The number seven had a symbolic significance in many ancient Near Eastern cultures, including Ugarit and Mesopotamia, as well as in the Old Testament. Some festivals lasted seven days (Tabernacles, Unleavened Bread), and the date of Pentecost is computed on the basis of seven times seven days. A seventh-day celebration is, therefore, not surprising. More puzzling is the fact that there seems to be no relationship between the week and the rest of the calendar.

One suggestion is that the Sabbath arose originally as a periodic day of observance unrelated to the lunar or solar cycle. For example, a market-day cycle of a fixed number of days is known in a variety of cultures, often from five to eight days in length and having nothing to do with the month or with other calendrical events. Nonetheless it has also been suggested that there may once have been a relationship between the week and the month. The seven-day week is intriguingly close to a quarter of a lunar month, suggesting that the Hebrew sabbath originated from a four-times-a-month celebration.

The Hebrew word 'sabbath' (*šābbāt*) is similar to the Akkadian *šapattu* or *sabattu* meaning 'full moon' or fifteenth day of the month. There are also the Babylonian menologies, a cycle of ominous days (*ūmê lemnūti*) which occurred four or five times a month, at approximately seven-day intervals. It is not clear that the *šapattu* is related to this cycle. If it were related, it would strengthen the argument that the Old Testament Sabbath is connected with Mesopotamia; if not, the suggestion remains mainly speculative. No Old Testament texts connect the Sabbath with the lunar cycle in any way.

The Annual Festivals

Most of Leviticus 23 is taken up with the annual festivals (*mô'ădîm*, 'appointed times'). (As noted above, the reference to the sabbath may be a secondary insertion.) These follow the agricultural year, most being related to specific events in the annual round of planting and harvesting. They all fall within the main growing period and avoid the winter months. Holy days were treated like the Sabbath—indeed, they may be referred to as '(annual) sabbaths'—with no work being done. One apparent difference from the weekly sabbath was that the preparation of food was allowed (cf. Exod. 12.16).

Passover and Unleavened Bread
Lev. 23.5 briefly mentions the Passover, but Leviticus is otherwise silent about this important celebration, with no details given. This may not be significant if there is a P document, since passages normally labelled P include lengthy descriptions of the observance, especially Exod. 12.1-20. In Leviticus, Passover is presupposed but is tied up with the Festival of Unleavened Bread (23.6-8), the seven-day period when only unleavened bread (*maṣṣôt*) was eaten and no leavening or leavened products were allowed in the land. The festival was inaugurated by the Passover meal, at which unleavened bread was eaten, on the evening between the fourteenth and fifteenth of Nisan. The first full day (fifteenth) and the last day (twenty-second) were holy days.

It is important to establish when the Passover became associated with the Feast of Unleavened Bread. Wellhausen argued that the D source was the first to show knowledge of the Passover which, in his opinion, had developed from the

offering of the firstlings of cattle. He believed that the Passover
was not mentioned in the early Pentateuchal sources (JE).
Apart from the doubt about whether such sources exist, it is
now generally admitted that some early traditions do mention
the Passover (Exod. 23.18, 34.25, for example). Firstlings are
nowhere associated with a fixed time of year, making
Wellhausen's thesis hypothetical. Haran argued that the
Passover was associated with Unleavened Bread from early
times and was so linked in all the biblical sources. However, his
argument that the Passover goes back to a 'nomadic' way of
life, with Unleavened Bread arising in settled conditions, must
be considered problematic in view of recent discussions about
nomadism and the Israelite settlement.

Haran also maintains that the Passover in Exodus 12 and
elsewhere is actually envisaged as a temple sacrifice. This is
indicated by hints and tensions in the text. These tensions, he
believes, were created when the author attempted, anachro-
nistically, to connect the Passover with the exodus, and was
obliged to transform the Passover of his own time into a hypothetical 'first Passover' in captivity in Egypt.

An important day within the festival of unleavened bread
was the Wave Sheaf (*'ōmer*) Day (23.9-14). On this day a
symbolic sheaf of grain was cut as the first fruits of the harvest
and presented before God. In addition, certain specific
offerings were enjoined: a male lamb as a burnt offering, a
cereal offering of two *ephahs* of flour mixed with oil, and a
quarter *hin* of wine as a drink offering. This ceremony
marked the start of the grain harvest. No bread or grain from
the new crop was to be eaten until the first sheaf had been
brought. The ceremony took place on the Sunday ('the day
after the sabbath') during the days of unleavened bread. In
later centuries, various sects disagreed over whether the 'day
after the sabbath' meant the day after the first annual sabbath
(the holy day on 15 Nisan) or after the weekly sabbath, the
most natural reading of the Hebrew text being that which
interpreted it as the weekly sabbath. This date also affected the
date of Pentecost.

Feast of Weeks or Pentecost

The spring grain harvest began on the Wave Sheaf Day and continued for seven weeks until the Feast of Weeks (Lev. 23.15-21). For some reason no specific term ('Feast of Weeks' or otherwise) occurs for this festival in Leviticus. The Feast of Weeks did not fall on a specific day of the month but was counted from the Wave Sheaf Day, reckoning seven sabbaths. The Feast of Weeks (*ḥag šāvu'ôt*, Exod. 34.22) was on the day after the seventh sabbath, called the fiftieth day when counting inclusively (that is, including both the starting and finishing day in the total). Hence, in later times the day was given the Greek name of *pentēkostē* 'fiftieth (day)', from which the English Pentecost comes.

From later Jewish sources, it is known that there was disagreement among the sects about the date of this festival. The dispute concerned whether seven weeks from a floating annual sabbath on 15 Nisan or seven sabbaths from the first day of the week should be counted, to arrive at another first day of the week. Some translations and lexicons render the Hebrew phrase *ševa' šabbātôt* as 'seven weeks', but this would be the only place where *šabbāt* means week in the Old Testament; it is more likely that the word means 'sabbath' here, as elsewhere. Only in Second Temple times did the meaning 'week' develop, allowing some sects to count from a fixed day of the month. Hebrew usage and later priestly practice indicate that Shavuot was always celebrated on a Sunday as long as the temple stood and only later became fixed on the sixth of Sivan as it is among most Jews today.

Shavuot also had its own specific offerings. Two loaves of bread were baked from flour made from the new grain and presented before God. Unusually, they were to be baked with leaven; this seems to be the only exception to the requirement that cereal offerings were to be unleavened, though nothing is said about their being burnt on the altar. Accompanying this were a burnt offering of seven lambs, a bull, and two rams; a sin offering of a male goat; and a well-being offering of two male lambs.

Day of Trumpets

The first day of the seventh month (Tishri) was a holy day
celebrated by the blowing of trumpets (Lev. 23.23-25). The
type of trumpet used is not specified. Another passage usually
associated with P mentions a set of silver trumpets to be used
for ceremonial occasions and in times of war (Num. 10.1-10).
These may be the same, but the symbolic blowing may not
have been confined to these. The ram's horn (*šôfār*) associated
with the festival in modern times may have been a later
development or interpretation, but there is no way of knowing.
Other than the blowing of trumpets and the command to do
no work, nothing further is stated about this day. Num. 29.1-5
lists sacrifices to be offered, though it is unclear why they are
omitted in Leviticus.

Day of Atonement

The tenth day of the seventh month was the Day of
Atonement (*yôm hakkippurîm*). Lev. 23.26-32 states that this
day was a time of no work and of fasting ('you shall afflict
your souls'), a time of holy convocation, and that an offering of
fire was to be made. No further data are given. Yet it is known
that the ceremony of the two goats was also associated with
this day, a ceremony which Leviticus 16 describes in detail.
Was the ceremony of Leviticus 16 once an independent
observance which only later became associated with the tenth
of Tishri? Most of that chapter gives no indication of when the
ceremony was to take place. Only towards the end of the
chapter (16.29-34) is the ritual connected with Day of
Atonement known from Leviticus 23.

Leviticus 16.1 connects ch. 16 back to the regulations about
the priests in chs. 8–10, linking it with the one proper occasion
when a priest (the high priest only) could appear before God in
the Holy of Holies itself. Whereas Nadab and Abihu had acted
improperly (though their sin is never specified) and had been
punished by death, the correct ceremony at the right time
could allow the priest to come into God's actual presence.

The central core of the ritual was the ceremony with two
goats. One goat was for God and one was for Azazel, the choice
being determined by lottery. 'Azazel' remains an enigma. No

explanation is found in the text of Leviticus 16, and the word does not occur elsewhere in the Old Testament or in early inscriptions. Various etymologies have been proposed, but none is compelling. Later Jewish tradition identified Azazel with the leader of the fallen angels (Grabbe). Although this identification itself may have originated through attempts to understand this passage, scholars have often proposed that Azazel represents some sort of demonic figure. This is suggested by the context as well as by later Jewish interpretation.

Before the high priest could come into God's presence, he first had to offer a bull as a sin offering for himself and his household. Then he went inside the veil and placed incense on the coals of his censer to make a cloud of smoke and hide the ark to protect himself from God who was seated on top of the ark. He sprinkled the blood of the bull on the ark, to atone for his own sins. Next, the goat for God was sacrificed and the blood sprinkled on the ark, which atoned for the holy place. The altar was atoned for by sprinkling on it blood from both the bull and goat.

The sins of the people were removed by the treatment of the goat for Azazel. It was not slain. Rather, the high priest laid hands on it and confessed the sins of the congregation, thus transferring them to its head. The goat was then taken away and sent into the wilderness, bearing away all the sins of Israel on its head. Finally, the high priest offered burnt offerings on behalf of the congregation and himself.

Feast of Booths
The Feast of Booths or Tabernacles (*sukkôt*) was the final festival of the year, celebrated after the autumn harvest (Lev. 23.33-36, 39-43) on 15–22 Tishri. It probably arose from the practice of farmers who would build a temporary shelter (booth) in the field to sleep in, enabling them to protect the harvest and make best use of the daylight until the harvest was gathered. The people were to take fruit, palm leaves, tree branches, and willows and make booths as a part of the celebration. The first and eighth days were holy days on which no work was to be done.

As with the Day of Trumpets, no sacrifices are listed for
Sukkot in Leviticus. At Num. 29.12-39, however, an elaborate
series of sacrifices was to take place, each of the eight days
having its own particular ceremony. This followed a
diminishing series, beginning with 13 bulls on the first day, 12
bulls on the second, and so on down to seven bulls on the
seventh day. Accompanying these were daily sacrifices of two
rams and 14 yearling lambs, plus cereal and drink offerings.
The eighth day had its own separate ceremony.

Sabbatical Year and Jubilee

Leviticus 25 describes two year-long observances: the seventh
or sabbatical year (year of release: *šĕmiṭṭāh*) and the jubilee
(*yôvēl*) year. A cycle of seven-year periods is envisaged, the
last year having the land left fallow with no crops sown.
Spontaneous growth was allowed, and the people could eat its
produce on a day-to-day basis, but no harvesting as such was
permitted. There would be no hardship, however, since the
land would miraculously produce enough in the sixth year to
tide the inhabitants over until the harvest of the crops sown in
the new cycle (Lev. 25.19-22).

In Leviticus the seventh year seemed to be primarily an
agricultural observance (cf. also Exod. 23.10-11). According to
some passages, however, loans and the enslavement of
Israelites were also cancelled in the seventh year (Deut. 15.1-
3, 12-15; Jer. 34.8-16). If so, the seventh year would have been
an integral part of the nation's life, with widespread
implications for the economy. On the other hand, there seems
to be a contradiction between Leviticus, which saw the year of
release as the jubilee, and other passages which ascribe release
to the sabbatical year (see below).

The tithing cycle prescribed in Deuteronomy is not mentioned in Leviticus (or other P passages) but, if a sabbatical
year existed, the tithes of Deuteronomy 14–15 would work
only if operated on a seven-year cycle. That is, the tithe of the
third year (Deut. 14.28-29) would have to be coordinated with
the seventh year, or it would sometimes fall in the sabbatical
year when tithing was not possible. Thus, the tithe of the third

year would have been paid in the third and sixth year out of the cycle rather than as part of an independent three-year cycle. On the matter of tithing in general, see Chapter 4.

The jubilee took place after seven sabbatical-year cycles. The text is somewhat ambiguous. On the one hand, the jubilee may have coincided with the last year of the seventh cycle (Lev. 25.8); on the other, it was explicitly stated to be the fiftieth year (Lev. 25.10-11). If this was so, it would mean two fallow years in a row, yet there is no mention of the effects of such a situation or how it was managed. The Jewish *Book of Jubilees* counts a jubilee cycle of forty-nine years, showing the 'fiftieth year' might be counted inclusively (including both the starting and finishing years in the calculation). It may be that this is what the author of Leviticus 25 had in mind, but the point is never clarified.

The jubilee was also a fallow year but, according to Leviticus, it was more than this; it was a year of release (Lev. 25; also Lev. 27.16-24; Num. 36.4). Land was to return to the family which originally owned it, and Israelite slaves were to be released. Agrarian land was considered an inalienable heritage granted by God, to be kept in the family in perpetuity. Therefore, the land could not be sold permanently. Any sale was viewed in effect as a long-term lease which reverted back to the family in the jubilee year. The sale price was determined according to the length of time to the next jubilee, with the purchaser paying for the number of crops obtained before it reverted to the original owners. That is, the closer to the jubilee, the less was paid. (Lev. 25.29-34 notes that town property was treated differently and could be transferred, without right of repossession, after a probation year in which the sellers could change their mind and redeem it.)

Slavery was accepted as an institution. Foreign slaves could be bought and sold as chattels (Lev. 25.44-46), although laws regulated how they were treated (see Deut. 21.10-14). But Israelites were not to be treated as slaves. If a person or family sold themselves because of debts or poverty, they were to be treated as hired servants, and in the jubilee they were allowed to go free.

On the question of the release of slaves and cancellation of

loans there is contradiction between Leviticus and other
passages, as already noted. Leviticus 25 and 27 are the only
descriptions of the jubilee year. Perhaps the jubilee was an
innovation on the part of the priestly writer, in an attempt to
replace some of the function of the current sabbatical year
with a new institution of the jubilee. This highlights the question of the antiquity of these institutions.

Comparison has been made with the Mesopotamian
mīšarum and the *andurāru* which go back to the Old Babylonian and Old Assyrian periods (early second millennium
BCE). An influential study on this question was written by H.
Lewy, who drew attention to these points: Babylonian
anduraru is cognate with the Hebrew *děrôr* 'release'. A king
would declare a *mišarum* which was a general declaration of
justice. He might also declare an *anduraru*, 'release', which
could include a remission of certain taxes, a release of debts,
reversion of property to its original owners, or manumission of
slaves. The *mišarum* might include one or more of these, but
not necessarily all of them. Such declarations are known to
have come from several kings of the second millennium BCE,
suggesting that it was common for a king to declare such a
'release' in the first year of his reign. Lewy argued that the
practice originated with the Amorites, and spread into
Mesopotamia and Israel, the Amorites often being supposed to
be among the ancestors of Israel. The Israelite innovation was
to declare a jubilee at regular intervals rather than in the first
year of a new reign, as in Mesopotamia.

The Akkadian evidence for the *mišarum* and *anduraru* is
generally accepted (cf. Finkelstein), but its interpretation in
relation to the Israelite institution is not straightforward.
Looking at both the biblical and the Mesopotamian evidence,
N.-P. Lemche found many instances of careless reasoning in
the comparisons made by Lewy and in other earlier studies.
For example, Old Testament material was used to interpret
the Old Babylonian, which was then used to interpret the
Israelite, with clear dangers of circular reasoning. The practice of a king's granting a release in his first year in the Old
Babylonian period proves nothing about the antiquity of the
jubilee in Israel which is, after all, somewhat different.

Lemche admits some evidence for the antiquity of a seventh fallow year in agriculture, but the development of a sabbatical year with all its social accoutrements seems late.

The existence of a sabbatical year is attested in historical sources of the Second Temple period (Grabbe). This included a rest from growing crops, at least from the time of the Maccabees (1 Macc. 6.49, 53; Josephus, *Ant.* 13.7.4–8.1 §§228–35; 14.16.2 §475). It is known from actual documents found in the Judaean Desert that the cancellation of debts and return of property in the seventh year was an accepted institution (Murabba'at 18; 24). There is no mention of the jubilee year, however, except in literature such as the *Book of Jubilees*. The indication is that the sabbatical year but not the jubilee was observed in Second Temple times. It is also reasonable to conclude that the seventh year was in some way observed in late post-exilic times, though how much further back it can be projected is a question. Whether the jubilee was ever observed is a matter of speculation.

Other Festivals?

The list of festivals in Leviticus 23 seems intended to be complete. No other celebrations are listed elsewhere in the Pentateuch, and no other sacred or holy festivals are known from later Judaism. Such celebrations as Purim (from Esther) and Hanukkah (from the time of the Maccabees) were taken up into the festival calendar of Judaism, but they have never had the same weight as the Old Testament festivals. They are not holy days as such and are not treated in the same way as the annual sabbaths.

In the Old Testament and elsewhere there are occasional references to other festivals, or what appear to be other festivals. For example, Elkanah made a yearly pilgrimage to Shiloh with his wives to make sacrifices, according to 1 Samuel 1. This could be interpreted as one of the great festivals known from the Pentateuch, or as an otherwise unknown festival. It was most likely a private family celebration with nothing to do with the required yearly festival calendar (Haran).

The Qumran Temple Scroll indicates that there was a Feast

of the Firstfruits of Oil, a Feast of the Firstfruits of Wine, and apparently, a Feast of the Wood Offering (11QT 19-25) in its cultic calendar. These may have been sectarian innovations, though scholars do not agree that the Temple Scroll is in fact a product of the Qumran community. However, Josephus mentions, in passing, a Festival of Woodgathering (*War* 2.17.6 §425; cf. Neh. 10.35). From the name and context, it seems to have been related to the bringing of wood for the altar to the temple. It is not clear that it was a holy day, like Purim and Hanukkah; the extant text of the Temple Scroll does not indicate that work was prohibited on the three feasts which are unique to it.

The most important suggestion about another festival in ancient Israel is that of the New Year. This festival is not mentioned as such, but a theory about it was developed by S. Mowinckel who argued that Israel began its new year in the autumn with the seventh month now called Tishri. This coincided with the wine harvest but acquired symbolic features concerned with the rule of God and of his representative, the earthly king. The rulership of the king was celebrated, perhaps with a ritual deposition from rule followed by re-enthronement. The kingship of Yahweh was also celebrated, with a ritual re-enthronement. Up to a third of the book of Psalms was thought to have originated from association with this celebration, including the royal psalms and the enthronement-of-Yahweh psalms.

This thesis was widely accepted in the past and is still influential among scholars today. Nevertheless, it has been criticized as follows:

1. Israel's new year may not have begun in the autumn. Clines has put forward a forceful argument that the normally attested time of new year in pre-exilic times was the spring. Admittedly, the beginning of the new year may not have been consistently observed everywhere in pre-exilic Israel, shifting from spring to autumn or vice versa at different times, and the two kingdoms of Israel and Judah may not always have used the same calendar. Nevertheless, there are cogent arguments for the belief that the most consis-

tent time for the beginning of the new year was in the spring; and the idea that reckoning from the spring was a post-exilic innovation certainly cannot be sustained.

2. No such festival is described in the surviving texts. Several celebrations are assigned to the seventh month (Day of Trumpets, Day of Atonement, Feast of Tabernacles), but none of these is specifically associated with a new year celebration. The Day of Trumpets marks the first day of the seventh month, but is not the primary festival which is adduced as support for the theory. Mowinckel focuses mainly on the Feast of Tabernacles, but this does not occur until the fifteenth of the month in the present festival calendar. Mowinckel assumes that present-day celebrations are remnants of an original festival which was also divided up and displaced from its original location.

3. No single psalm or other writing contains all the elements (ritual dethronement and re-enthronement of the king, proclamation of God's kingship, and so on) hypothesized to be a part of the Israelite festival liturgy.

4. The main analogy for the Israelite new year festival is that of the *akitu* festival in Babylon; however, the evidence for that festival is very late, from the Seleucid period. Although it may have been celebrated earlier, there are no details to be used in evaluating the Old Testament material. Also, the Babylonian festival was celebrated, not in the autumn, but in spring. Yet no one has attempted to connect the new year with Passover or Unleavened Bread which were spring festivals in Israel.

Thus, if there was such a new year festival as hypothesized, it has been largely forgotten or suppressed in the surviving literature, somewhat different celebrations having been substituted for it. These arguments against Mowinckel's theory seem decisive to me, but others argue in favour of his thesis. (See J. Day who evaluates it positively.)

Further Reading

On general calendar matters, see:

J. Finegan, *A Handbook of Biblical Chronology* (Princeton: Princeton University Press, 1964).

D.J.A. Clines, 'The Evidence for an Autumnal New Year in Pre-Exilic Israel Reconsidered', *JBL* 93 (1974), pp. 22-40.

—'New Year', *IDBSup* (1976), pp. 625-29.

J. van Goudoever, *Biblical Calendars* (Leiden: Brill, 1961).

A major study of the sabbath is found in:

N.-E.A. Andreasen, *The Old Testament Sabbath* (SBL Dissertation 7; Missoula: Scholars Press, 1972).

B.E. Shafer, 'Sabbath', *IDBSup* (1976), pp. 760-62.

For a discussion of the Passover, see:

M. Haran, *Temples and Temple-Service in Ancient Israel* (Oxford: Clarendon Press, 1978), pp. 317-48.

For a history of the interpretation of the scapegoat ritual, see:

L.L. Grabbe, 'The Scapegoat Ritual: A Study in Early Jewish Interpretation', *JSJ* 18 (1987), pp. 152-67.

On the sabbatical year and jubilee, see:

L.L. Grabbe, 'Maccabean Chronology: 167–164 or 168–165 BCE?', *JBL* 110 (1991), pp. 59-74; the sabbatical year in Second Temple times is discussed on pp. 60-63.

J.J. Finkelstein, 'Amiṣaduqa's Edict and the Babylonian "Law Codes" ', *JCS* 15 (1961), pp. 91-104.

N.-P. Lemche, 'The Manumission of Slaves—the Fallow Year—the Sabbatical Year—the Jobel Year', *VT* 26 (1976), pp. 38-59.

—'*Andurārum* and *Mīšarum*: Comments on the Problem of Social Edicts and their Application in the Ancient Near East', *JNES* 38 (1979), pp. 11-22.

H. Lewy, 'The Biblical Institution of *Dᵉrôr* in the Light of Akkadian Documents', *EI* 5 (1958), pp. 21*-31*.

R. North, *The Sociology of the Biblical Jubilee* (AnBib 4; Rome: Pontifical Biblical Institute, 1954).

On the festivals from the Temple Scroll, see:

Y. Yadin (ed.), *The Temple Scroll: Hebrew and English* (3 vols. in 4; Jerusalem: Israel Exploration Society, 1983).

For a sympathetic discussion of Mowinckel's thesis, see:

J. Day, *Psalms* (Old Testament Guide Series; Sheffield: JSOT Press, 1990).

7

THE CONTINUING
RELEVANCE OF LEVITICUS

IN SPITE OF ITS ALIEN character to modern readers—at least, at first glance—Leviticus has been a source of much theological meaning and an object of hermeneutical interest from the earliest times in known Jewish history to the present. Questions of meaning and interpretation have been taken up in previous chapters. Some of the points made elsewhere are reviewed here, and we shall look at examples of the ways in which the book has been interpreted and applied over the centuries in Judaism and Christianity. It is difficult to limit discussions to Leviticus alone since interpreters often address themselves to themes which cut across more than one book. General matters of the cult and temple may therefore be considered, regardless of whether every detail is found specifically in Leviticus.

However ideologized the book of Leviticus may have been, it most likely bore some resemblance to the actual cult and practice of religion in Israel, at least in Second Temple times and probably much earlier. Any regulations regarded as authoritative were naturally important for cult practice while the temple stood. Once the temple was in ruins, however, cultic discussion could be only theoretical. This observation sets the programme for the subsequent use of the book in both Judaism and Christianity. The Jews could not apply much of the book directly because there was no temple, and the Christians had come to reject not only the temple but also much of the 'ceremonial law'—especially the instructions about clean and unclean animals, purity and pollution, and the like. Instead of the book's reflecting the symbolic system present in the sanctuary and cult, it became the focus of great symbolic interest in itself.

The symbolic interpretation of the book had begun well before the destruction of the Second Temple. An important example of this is the Temple Scroll (11QT). This recasts many of the laws in Exodus to Deuteronomy. Sometimes it represents a fairly exact quotation of what is known from our present Masoretic text, but the material is often quite different in detail, though similar in substance; above all, everything was given a new context. The result is a document which envisages a sanctuary and cult different from that usually extracted from the Pentateuch, and different from what little is known of the actual cult contemporary with the Temple Scroll.

As far as can be established, the contents were meant to be applied literally, if the writers of 11QT were ever to gain control of the Jerusalem temple (or set up their own temple). Moreover, the document seems to represent certain ideals of the writers which allow an insight into their view of the sacred and into their theological concerns in general. For example, not just the temple but the whole city was holy. Latrines were kept at a distance of 3,000 cubits, which meant that they could not be visited on the sabbath because they were more than the permitted sabbath day's journey away from the city.

Philo of Alexandria (c. 20 BCE to 50 CE) is one of the best-known Jewish exegetes of antiquity, most of his voluminous writings being extant. Philo's method was to expound on two levels: first, what he calls the 'literal' meaning (though this often represents a stage of interpretation, as we would see it), then—far more importantly to him—the spiritual or allegorical meaning. The text is filled with symbols relating to the nature of God, the progress of the human soul toward perfection, and the virtues and vices, to name only a few of the most important.

Most of Philo's commentaries are on the book of Genesis, but in the *Special Laws* (*De specialibus legibus*) he explores the meaning of the legal sections of the Pentateuch, including many of the laws in Leviticus. Matters relating to sacrifice are found primarily in Book I. Philo sees the universe as God's temple, 'having for its sanctuary the most sacred part of all existence, even heaven, for its votive ornaments the stars, for its priests the angels' (1.66). The priest presiding at the altar was to be physically whole, a symbol of the perfection of the soul (1.80). As the animals offered were to be unblemished, so the worshipper was to approach the altar with no blemish or infirmity of the soul (1.167). And so on for every element within the sacrificial ritual.

The washing of the entrails and legs of the burnt offering before putting these parts on the altar (Lev. 1.9), for example, is a small detail which an interpreter might easily overlook. To Philo this act, like all others, has great significance (1.206-207). The entrails or belly signify lust which must be washed away, along with the pollutions from drunkenness and gluttony which affect lives negatively. Washing the legs indicates that the steps of the person should no longer be on the earth but in the upper air. The abode of the soul which loves God is to be celestial, not terrestrial.

The image of the universe as God's temple has important consequences for Philo's discussion of the high priest's garments which are also a symbol of the universe (1.84-97). The blue of the tunic is a symbol of the air. The breastplate represents heaven, the two shoulder pieces representing the two hemispheres, one above the earth and one underneath it. The twelve stones on the chest (which correspond to the tribes of Israel in the original text) stand for the signs of the zodiac. The decorations on the hem of the skirt symbolize earth and water, while the bells attached there are models of the harmony and unity of the universe. The priest was to meditate on the imagery of his garments and so live a life worthy of this cosmic message.

Philo's younger contemporary Josephus, the Jewish historian (37–c.100 CE), does not usually interpret explicitly but paraphrases the biblical text. Nevertheless, there is a great deal of subtle interpretation taking place. An example concerns the tabernacle and the dress of the high priest which Josephus explains in an allegorical manner similar to that of

Philo (*Ant.* 3.7.7. §§179–87). The two writers may have been dependent on a common tradition, though it is conceivable that Josephus knew some of Philo's writings.

Christian interpretation of the temple and cult began in early times. Although Christians initially continued to participate fully in temple worship, with time they came to see it as inessential or even to reject it outright. The process of spiritualizing sacrifices and other temple service thus began in the New Testament itself, though to what extent this happened before the destruction of the temple is difficult to say since most New Testament literature is post-70 CE.

There is a surprising number of references to Leviticus in the New Testament—over one hundred quotations or direct citations. All the Old Testament sacrifices, as well as much else, were seen as representing Christ. Christ was the 'paschal lamb' (1 Cor. 5.7). The shedding of his blood was analogous to that shed at the altar (Heb. 9.12, 22). He was even referred to explicitly as a sin offering in 1 Jn 2.2 and 4.10, depending on how the Greek *hilasmos* was translated.

One of the richest sources of such interpretation is the epistle to the Hebrews, which draws openly on the cult for many of its symbols. Christ was the heavenly high priest, presiding over the celestial temple. Like the earlier high priest, he offered sacrifice for sin, but here—in an ironic switch of metaphor—he offers not a substitute victim but himself. He is both officiating priest and sacrifice on the altar (7.27). The arrangement of the tabernacle and the ceremonies within it are followed almost verse by verse in Hebrews 9 (although the arrangement of furniture in the inner sanctum seems to differ from that in the Old Testament). The book of the Hebrews is impossible to understand without a thorough knowledge of the Pentateuch.

Early patristic literature continues in the same vein. Origen (c. 185–254 CE), like Philo, interpreted on both the literal and allegorical levels. Preserved among his writings are a series of *Homilies on Leviticus* in which he saw deep significance in the smallest details of the sacrificial system. For example, the fifth part added for the reparation of a holy object wrongly used (Lev. 5.14-16) is interpreted 'literally' as five parts plus an additional one (that is, restoration of 220 per cent!) because of the particular Greek word used (Origen depended on the Septuagint text for the basis of his exegesis). Allegorically, it refers to the five senses in his opinion, in particular to the five 'spiritual senses' (*Hom. in Lev.* 3.6-7).

Contemporary with the early patristic literature was the rabbinic literature. Although the bulk of this arose after the destruction of the temple, much theoretical discussion about the operation of the cult is found in rabbinic writings. This begins in the Mishnah and continues unabated in the two talmuds and the midrashim, and a substantial portion of it is derived from Leviticus. Such cultic discussion became a prime metaphor for rabbinic Jews, forming an important means by which they created a new cosmology as a way of understanding the world in which they lived and integrating themselves into it. The precise structure of this world view may be debatable, but one who has spent a great deal of effort trying to understand it is Jacob Neusner. In his commentary on the Mishnah and subsequent publications on the Tannaitic Midrashim and other works, he suggested how the writers of these documents understood their tradition and how they used it as a tool for self-identification.

In Neusner's view, those who discussed and developed the various elements of ritual purity were coming to terms with a world which had changed vastly after the destruction of the temple. To an outsider, much of the debate seems to be squabbling over picayune legal details of texts which could not be applied anyway, now that the temple no longer existed, but this is far from the truth. Neusner describes the importance of the debate as follows (pp. 282-83):

> The Mishnah's evidence presents a Judaism which at its foundations and through all of its parts deals with a single fundamental question: What can a man do? The evidence of the Mishnah points to a Judaism which answers that question simply: Man, like God, makes the world work... The Mishnah's Judaism is a system built to celebrate that power of man to form intention, willfully to make the world with full deliberation, in entire awareness, through decision and articulated intent. So does the Mishnah assess the condition of Israel, defeated and helpless, yet in its Land:

without power, yet holy; lacking all focus, in no particular
place, certainly without Jerusalem, yet set apart from the
nations. This message of the Mishnah clashes with a reality
itself cacophonous, full of dissonance and disorder. The
evidence of the Mishnah points to a Judaism defiant of the
human condition of Israel, triumphant over the
circumstance of subjugation and humiliation, thus
surpassing all reality.

Far from being a 'religion of pots and pans', rabbinic Judaism
used the various ritual and cultic regulations—many of
which no longer had practical meaning apart from the
temple—to make a profound statement about God, the world,
and themselves.

An example of how a particular tradition of Leviticus was
interpreted is the ceremony with the two goats on the Day of
Atonement (Grabbe). As noted in Chapter 6 the original
meaning of the 'goat for Azazel' is uncertain, but it very
quickly became assimilated to the demonic tradition. In the
Enochic literature, one of the leaders of the fallen angels is a
figure called Asael. He became identified with Azazel, and this
identification was in turn combined with the Satanic tradition
which included not only the 'Adversary' of the Old Testament
texts but also the figure of Belial known from Qumran and
other Jewish texts. In the light of this interpretation, the goats
were seen as one for God and one (the scapegoat) for Satan.

Not surprisingly, Christian tradition as represented by the
early patristic writers took a different view. They may
indicate some actual knowledge of the ceremony as it was
conducted in the last days of the Second Temple; however that
may be, they interpreted *both* goats as a type of Christ. The
slain goat represented the slain son of God, and the goat
released into the wilderness represented the Christ who bears
the sins of the world. In one Christian text, however, the
scapegoat seems to be a representative of the devil (Rev. 20).

When modern Jews and Christians are asked what the
book means, a variety of answers are given. It is common to
find some of the laws of Leviticus interpreted as medical or
health regulations, with the view that if the dietary and
'hygienic' rules of the Pentateuch were carefully followed,
many modern diseases would be eliminated (cf. S.I. McMillen,

None of These Diseases). It is doubtful whether many doctors would follow this advice, and it is has been shown that hygiene is unlikely to be the source of the regulations. Nevertheless, this is another example of how the ancient text is still found meaningful by some modern readers and interpreters.

Certain contemporary concerns which need not be religious have been indicated by recent or forthcoming publications of J. Milgrom. He argued that the main focus for the command that all slaughter be at the altar was concern for animal life and welfare. By restricting the opportunities for slaughter, the need for rational and compassionate use of animals for food would be brought to the attention of the Israelites. In another article, Milgrom deals with the question of ecology and apparently shows that the priestly writers already had an ecological concern in embryonic form.

Yet the cultic concerns of ancient Israel are still alive today among Jews both religious and secular. J.Z. Smith has shown how the themes of land, exile, temple, and sacred centre have sustained Jews and Judaism up to the present. (With a little mental adjustment, many of these concerns can be applied to contemporary Christian thought.) The land has been a vital symbol to Judaism since the time of ancient Israel. Other lands were polluted; in Israel even the mundane and the everyday became in some way sanctified. In words ascribed to R. Zeira, 'Even the ordinary conversation of the people of the Land of Israel requires study' (*Genesis Rabba* 34.7)—daily chit-chat becomes Torah in the Holy Land! The concept of sacred space pervades this thinking. At the centre of the sacred area was the temple itself, the navel of the earth, the divine abode—with God himself seated on Zion, the highest mountain in the world.

Much of Jewish history has been the story of exile from that land and temple; nevertheless, what was not inhabited in the flesh was still peopled in spirit. The Jewish mystical tradition overcame this separation from the temple—the centre—by means of the concepts of sacred space and time (Scholem). The sabbath in particular is a moment when time and distance are abolished and the earthly and heavenly temples are immediately accessible in the living room of every Jewish home. Myth overcomes reality; myth has created a new reality. The temple and its ritual are cosmic activities. The shedding of the blood of bulls and goats exposes the very heart of existence, bringing creation and the eschaton together in a single moment.

This survey was intended to be allusive, not to give a full review of how Leviticus has been interpreted over the centuries. Its purpose has been to hint to the modern Jew or Christian the rich theological and religious resources available in a work even so apparently arcane as Leviticus. The book is part of the Christian and Jewish religious heritage, a canonical text taking its place beside other books of the Hebrew Bible as a hermeneutical source. The renewal of interest in Leviticus is long overdue.

Further Reading

For Philo and Josephus, see the translations in the Loeb Classical Library:

F.H. Colson *et al.* (eds.), *Philo* (12 vols.; LCL; Cambridge, MA: Harvard, 1929–53).

H.St.J. Thackeray *et al.* (eds.), *Josephus* (9 vols.; LCL; London: Heinemann, 1926–65).

For the interpretation of the scapegoat ritual in later Judaism, see:

L.L. Grabbe, 'The Scapegoat Ritual: A Study in Early Jewish Interpretation', *JSJ* 18 (1987), pp. 152-67.

On the epistle to the Hebrews, see:

H.W. Attridge, *The Epistle to the Hebrews* (Hermeneia; Philadelphia: Fortress Press, 1989).

Origen's interpretation of Leviticus can be found especially in:

M. Borret (ed.), *Origène: Homélies sur le Lévitique* (2 vols.; SC 286-87; Paris: Cerf, 1981).

On Jewish interpretation of Leviticus from rabbinic times to now, the following are helpful:

J. Neusner, *Judaism: The Evidence of the Mishnah* (Chicago: Chicago University Press, 1981).

—*A Religion of Pots and Pans? Modes of Philosophical and Theological Discourse in Ancient Judaism: Essays and a Program* (BJS 156; Atlanta: Scholars Press, 1988).

G.G. Scholem, *On the Kabbalah and its Symbolism* (London: Routledge & Kegan Paul, 1965), esp. pp. 139-50.

J.Z. Smith, 'Earth and Gods', *History of Religions* 49 (1969), pp. 103-27, reprinted in *Map is not Territory: Studies in the History of Religions* (SJLA 23; Leiden: Brill, 1978), pp. 104-28.

INDEXES

INDEX OF REFERENCES

INDEX OF AUTHORS